# You Don't Have
## Who You Are to Have a

### Great
## Marriage

---

## The Power of the New Breakthrough
## *Marriage Blueprint™ Method*

---

# DR. MAX VOGT

New York

# YOU DON'T HAVE TO CHANGE WHO YOU ARE
## TO HAVE A GREAT MARRIAGE

Copyright ©2007 Dr. Max Vogt

ISBN: 1-60037-172-8 (Paperback)

Published by:

Knowledge Exchange Press
An Imprint of Morgan James Publishing
1225 Franklin Ave Ste 325
Garden City, NY 11530-1693
Toll Free 800-485-4943

Cover and Interior Design by:
Michelle Radomski
One to One Creative Services
www.creativeones.net

Habitat for Humanity®
Peninsula
Building Partner

*This book is for Pam, the love of my life.*

---

*Thank you Carolyne Givens for all your hard work editing,*
*For your generosity, and for the wisdom of your good eye*
*and good heart.*

*And thank you David Garfinkel for your skillful shepherding.*

# HIGH PRAISE

## for Dr. Max's **New Breakthrough** *Marriage Blueprint*™ **Method!**

**"Working with Dr. Max brought our marriage back from the brink of disaster…"**

"Working with Dr. Max brought our marriage back from the brink of disaster. Believing our marriage was destined for divorce court; we bickered loudly and publicly, and argued constantly. With his help, we discovered that what we bring to the relationship defines it, and we got the tools to make the relationship we truly wanted: a supportive, animated marriage where communication and intimacy flourish, rather than the doomed relationship we had and were continuing to create.

"With Dr. Max's tools, we are now able to work on improving our marriage on a daily basis. We enjoy one another's company, we communicate openly, we see each other as dynamic changing beings, and we do things together again (even dancing). By learning how to accept each other as we are rather than attempting to change one another as we used to, our marriage has dramatically and permanently improved."

—*Dan and Peggy T.*

**"I have a new pride, a new respect for and from my wife, a whole new attitude and approach to life."**

"Working with Dr. Max saved my marriage. When things seemed irreparable and hopeless, at times when many couples would have come apart permanently, my wife and I stayed to keep working with Dr. Max together because the work was deeply relevant to each of us as individuals. We trusted Dr. Max because he'd been right about us so many times, and so we lowered our defenses and opened up. Once I finally let it happen, examining my beliefs, and where they came from, and how they served me rapidly transformed my thinking about marriage, career, money, kids—even what I'm here for.

"I have a new pride, a new respect for and from my wife, a whole new attitude and approach to life. Our marriage is what we expect it to be, and I'm so happy when my wife shows me in so many ways that she expects it to be a lasting source of joy, fun, love, partnership and under-standing. We appreciate each other now more than we ever have. We know we have the skills and the tools to get through anything together."

—*Chuck S.*

**"Dr. Max helped me understand that my low expectations were keeping me from the marriage I deeply wanted ... I had been afraid that the differences would pull us apart. Through work with Dr. Max, I came to understood how this attitude was actually blocking intimacy—and killing the passionate energy our relationship originally had."**

"During the process of saving my marriage and family, Dr. Max helped me fundamentally change my thoughts and beliefs about intimate relationships and marriage.

"Before we started seeing Dr. Max, I remember asking with regard to my marriage, 'Is this all there is?' I thought that I would be happy if I could just work to accept how it was. However, when our marriage entered into crisis, Dr. Max helped me understand that my low expectations were keeping me from the marriage I deeply wanted.

"I used to think that I understood all there was to know about my husband, but his affair blew up that faulty notion. Dr. Max challenged me to get to know my husband as a new person each day. I worked to stop making assumptions about him, and this allowed for his growth and change. To my delight, I am finding that I actually like my husband more than I did when I thought I knew all about him!

"Dr. Max helped me to see how I was giving up my individuality and sense of self in my efforts to "make the marriage work." I had been afraid that the differences would pull us apart. Through work with Dr. Max, I came to understood how this attitude was actually blocking intimacy—and killing the passionate energy our relationship originally had."

—*Melinda B.*

"... the exercise about lowering our defenses has improved our marriage already."

"This Marriage book is a definitely must read for all married couples, or anyone thinking about getting married. Dr. Max gets right to the point in a no-nonsense, yet fun way! The strategies in the book are powerful, while being amazingly simple and easy to apply. In particular, the exercise about lowering our defenses has improved our marriage already! Thanks, Dr. Max."

—*Annie and Roger K.*

"We feel really relieved and happy that great marriages are doable, and not a fantasy, and now we have such a great and understandable roadmap for getting there."

"Dear Dr. Max: I have finished the book twice and am just starting to write out my beliefs. The reason I read it twice was because I just couldn't believe that the methods for identifying your beliefs and changing them and having a great marriage could be so easy. I thought I must be missing something. I've always been told (especially in my college course on psychology) that marriage counseling is the hardest thing to do because no one really knows what makes marriages tick. This approach to changing your marriage is easy and interesting. My wife and I have been discussing the Marriage Blueprints with our friends all this last week and we all feel we have a new and freeing way to approach our marriages. We feel really relieved and happy that great marriages are doable, and not a fantasy, and now we have such a great and understandable roadmap for getting there. Thanks for your help, Dr. Max."

—*Michael P.*

"My husband Jim is back! It's like a miracle!"

"My husband Jim is back! The great, wonderful man I once knew (who I thought had turned into a zombie) came back into the marriage after reading your book. He told me that he couldn't believe it was so simple to just do your methods. Jim has always been leery of therapists because he feared getting "ganged up on" by the counselor and me. He doesn't feel that way at all with your book and your approach.

He feels like you really explained how we all need to be understood and respected, and likes your view of marriage.

"I can't believe that he got into your book and that now we are really talking for the first time since we married 31 years ago. Jim seems like a new man after reading your book. You can see it in his face. He told me he's feeling that we really can be happily married and he wants to work on the marriage with me now. I am very appreciative of what he has done for himself and for me! Thank you for helping me get my husband and marriage back. It's like a miracle!"

—*Gina S.*

**"I feel more confident with Paula than I ever have, and happier being my own man in marriage without having to act macho at all."**

"I used to think I could never get it right with my wife and that women were impossible to understand. I thought it was some huge mystery about what would make her happy. Now I know that it's much simpler than I thought. Your book helped my wife Paula and me know how to make our marriage a great one; and in no uncertain terms that all we need to do is the straightforward methods you showed us. I feel more confident with Paula than I ever have, and much happier being my own man in marriage without having to act macho at all.

"Thank you for this wise and helpful book. My buddy asked me about it and I said, 'It's OK.' In my neighborhood, that's code for 'it's great!'."

—*Jack L.*

# TABLE OF CONTENTS

# TABLE OF CONTENTS (CONTINUED)

# FOREWORD

## by Michael and Dawn Angier

This may be the clearest, most useful book on relationships yet written. *You Don't Have to Change Who You Are to Have a Great Marriage* is an incredible opportunity for anyone who wants to truly have a great marriage.

As Dr. Max says, "No one can tell you what a great marriage is! You have to find out for yourself. I don't care how great or wonderful your therapist, guru, pastor, counselor or television personality is. They don't know the answer! I don't know the answer. All I can do is show you how to find the answer for yourself!"

And that's exactly what he does.

Dr. Max takes you step by step through a series of questions and strategies to uncover and clarify your Marriage Blueprint. He describes how your Marriage Blueprint "shows up" in the areas of sex, parenting, money, personal development and religion/spirituality in your marriage and family.

Michael and I experience the wonderful challenge of loving, living and working together. After reading Dr. Max's profile of our Marriage Blueprint, we more fully understand how to use this information to enhance our already powerful and satisfying marriage.

This book is for everyone who wants to be the best they can be for themselves and for their loved ones because all relationships start with YOU first!

We can all be grateful to Dr. Max for opening his office and sharing his 25 years of wisdom with us.

*—Michael and Dawn Angier*
http://SuccessNet.org
http://PresentationsMadeSimple.com

# PART ONE

The Intimacy Paradox
What Creates a Great Marriage?
Why So Many People Are Miserable in Theirs,
And How You Can Discover Untapped Resources
And Re-Ignite Passion and Intimacy in Yours

# CHAPTER ONE

## "How Neal and Rita Got Back Their Vital Marriage Hopes"

## (By Discovering Two *Never-Before-Revealed MARRIAGE SECRETS)*

Neal and Rita scrutinized me like an exotic bug as I opened the waiting room door to invite them in for their marriage therapy appointment.

They were a good-looking physically fit couple in their forties, but with an obvious burden of bitter pain on their hearts and souls from years of conflict and distress. You learn to see these things instantly—it showed in every part of who they were, despite their fine-muscled frames and sharp dress code.

It always tears at me, because I know that 95% of their suffering is totally unnecessary, but they don't know that yet.

The thrill for me is going to be like extracting the thorn from their sides and watching the relief flood over them. The nervous growl in the pit of my stomach is fear for them that they will say "no thanks," and stick it out with their misery.

*(Remember this story? A man was pounding on his thumb with a hammer. His friend said, "Why are you doing that?" He said, "Because it feels so good when I STOP!")*

Neal and Rita's faces carried that combination of hope and pessimism that I've seen in clients' eyes for 25 years now, and which even after all these years never fails to get my juices going.

What I have in store for them, they have never even heard of before—*will they be able to get the mental confusion out of their heads?* I sure hope so, because if they do, a real treat awaits them. If not, it's a lifetime of misunderstanding and silent desperation, and never knowing the joy of a great marriage.

I wonder, which will it be for Neal and Rita?

"Dr. Max, I presume," Neal said with a half smile and half grimace. Rita sneered at him and snorted out a little grunt of contempt. Did she used to love his little jokes and now had ended up hating them—and him? I would bet on it.

"That's me. Come on in and let's find out how to get you some answers and results as quickly as possible."

**Their hope** came from their own inner desires and longings for a great marriage. They want to achieve the dream of true marriage happiness; they are entitled to it, just as you are! Fortunately, it isn't difficult—no matter where you are coming from.

**Their pessimism** came from hearing so many stories of people who had attempted marriage therapy and whose relationships got even worse. I think marriage therapists and counselors have let you down in the past miserably, and I will to give you something that can produce powerful, positive changes very rapidly.

"Who is this guy?" they were naturally asking themselves.

"Does he know what he is doing? I know our friends liked him and they told us his new methods immediately improved their marriage, but will he be able to understand OUR situation and help us out? Does he really believe in marriage or helping people—or is he just doing it for the money? Will he be able to help us (maybe where others have failed)?"

**The answer is a resounding YES. But it has to be the right kind of therapy. The way is narrow, and this is the door. It's a door of perception. Many don't even see the door. You'll see it. Walk through it and everything changes. Stay on this side of it and nothing changes.**

More importantly, NO ONE can know your marriage like you do. You are the experts on your marriage, not me, not anyone else. My whole job is to help you be a better expert on YOUR marriage—a better self-coach, a better detective into your own mind and heart, and a better partner, using what you ALREADY know, but supercharging it!

Neal and Rita had been married 19 years, and as often happens, they really should have come to see me many years ago (12 years ago, in their case, when Rita had an affair)—but as the saying goes, you don't go when you oughta, you go when you must!

As I always do, I asked them immediately what **RESULTS** they wanted from our session.

They tried—like most people do—to start telling me the story of their misfortune and pain, their litany of complaints about each other, their reasons for hurting and the ways their partner had let them down. They each tried to get in their licks on each other as the source of their suffering.

---

*Secret #1: Reviewing your painful past only works if you know WHY you are doing it and FOR WHAT! Otherwise, why rehearse all the suffering?*

*Secret #2: There is almost NEVER any reason to go back and review the painful past anyway!*

---

I continued. "It is understandable that you want to review the past—it comes up from the pain of feeling misunderstood—but it is a terrible trap, and one which is so slippery that close to 100% of people fall right into it, go nowhere, and just howl down there in the pit of confusion and pain, bloodied and feeling alone.

Plenty of time for that, if you really want to talk about all of that after we start getting you the results and changes you want. Let's get the changes first and then if you still want to sit around blaming each other, be my guest. But not on my time, please."

Not to be deterred, each attempted to "try" each other in the "court of therapy." He does this, she does that, you've been there. "Your Honor, my opponent is responsible for the damages and is the source of my suffering and pain, I'm owed an apology. IT IS NOT MY FAULT!"

*This hogwash goes on all the time in therapists' offices* and many counselors actually allow it because they believe in "expression of feelings." If this happens to you, run like the wind, as fast as you can.

I interrupted. "OK, stop that, both of you, or get out of my office. Rita, what RESULTS do you want? Let's start with you."

I have had to *fire* some clients when they absolutely refused to work on their own behalf!

While they fumed and snarled at each other, I felt the enormous sadness and weight that comes sweeping over me when I see good people—smart people, loving people—caught in these traps of confusion and pain.

So much wasted energy, so much wasted effort. Enough, already!

Finally, after I had stopped them from **sharking** each other four times, Rita finally answered. "I just want to be trusted and not have to keep defending myself and explaining every single thing I do. I feel completely stifled and smothered by Neal. I want to feel happy and relaxed at home with Neal and our kids. I'm different from him in a lot of ways. I love him a lot, but I don't think he even likes me at all."

"Fair enough, Rita. Let me ask you this. Are you trustworthy?"

"Yes," she glared at me.

"Well, then why do you defend yourself and explain every single thing you do?"

"I feel I have to."

"Maybe you don't have to. Would it be all right with you if I showed you ways to be even more clear, honest and straight-forward than you already are, and if I showed you how to get out from under that smothering you talked about, and helped you feel happy and relaxed at home, would those be great goals?"

"Sure," she smiled. "You gonna give Neal a brain transplant?"

"No, Rita, *I'm going to give YOU a brain transplant,* or better said, I'm going to open up the doors in your brain you already closed, so you don't have to wait for Neal to get a brain transplant."

"OK, but I still think he's the one pushing me down."

"Wait just a damn minute," Neal started in.

"Hey Neal, I don't need any help doing my job here," I smiled at him, not totally friendly.

"Rita," I asked, "Do you really believe it's Neal who is pushing you down?"

"Yes, I do."

"What if I showed you that this thing you are describing, of Neal smothering you, is *a puppet show entirely put on by you?* Wouldn't that make you in charge of it?"

"Yes, that would make me in charge of it. But how can I be in control of Neal's actions? Isn't it true that you can't make someone do something they don't want to do? The whole idea infuriates me."

"That's true," I nodded my head. "Here's the secret to all that. I'm going to tell you a secret that almost no one knows, but if you understand it, your goals are going to be met and much sooner than you think. Ready?"

"Yes, I guess."

"You guess or you do? We don't have to go on here. I'm OK with stopping if you aren't interested."

"I am interested. Or I wouldn't be here," Rita snapped. I wondered if she would care to hear what I was about to say. It was going to blow her cover—the cover of holding Neal responsible for her unhappiness in her marriage.

"Here it is. It has two parts. It's going to be easy to understand but maybe a little hard to agree with:

**"First, that the marriage that you have right here, right now is exactly the marriage you expect to have. It's built exactly to the specifications of the blueprint you have in your head.**

**"Second, that the marriage you long to have is almost immediately obtainable, if you both want it, just by throwing a switch inside your head."**

Rita looked at the floor with such intensity that I thought she might be boring a hole with her eyes that she could crawl into and disappear.

Suddenly she looked up and growled at me, "Are you making fun of me?"

"Not at all."

"Are you saying that I deliberately set up all this conflict and pain and that I'm the problem?"

"Rita, I'm saying there *is no problem.* No, I'm not saying you deliberately set up anything. And I'm not saying you did this alone. I'd be saying exactly the same thing to Neal, and will be, the instant I start talking to him."

"Dr. Max, are you saying we are a couple of nut cases that created our own house of misery? That all this fighting, disagreeing and hurt feelings are all in our heads? What are you saying? I'm feeling confused by all of this, and how it's supposed to help us have a better marriage."

"Well, you remember that you said you wanted to be different. You wanted to be yourself and feel more at home with Neal. You wanted to feel more relaxed, and even clearer about expressing yourself, and that would be, in your opinion, a better marriage?"

"Yes, I remember that."

"Well, I'd really like to help you achieve those goals, starting right away, and I'm very serious about that. Do you believe that could happen today, Rita?"

"I believe in miracles."

"That's great! I used to doubt the existence of miracles, but I have seen so many happen with the couples I work with that I couldn't afford to doubt anymore. Now I know miracles happen all the time, and I don't see any reason you couldn't have one here today, do you?"

"Heck no. Go for it!" Now she was having a little more fun.

"Well, here's the way to start working on that. First of all, I want you to see that you have two different models of marriage, or as I call them, Marriage Blueprints, in conflict with one another."

"The first is a Marriage Blueprint inside of you that calls for marriage to be a struggle, a fight, and a contest of wills…"

"Can I say something?" Neal asked. "That *Blueprint*, as you call it, that's the one we both saw in our homes. Both Rita's parents and mine did exactly that—struggle, fight and compete against each other all the time. That's exactly what we said we would never do, and yet here we are doing exactly what we said we wouldn't do!"

"That's right," Rita agreed, nodding wide-eyed. "That's exactly it, just like we said, we can't believe we became our parents, just like we vowed we wouldn't. How did that happen?"

"There are two *Blueprints* active and often struggling inside each of us, one I call the **Family Marriage Blueprint,** and the other the **Personal Marriage Blueprint.** For most of us, these are fighting for dominance. This is exactly what's happening in your marriage."

"OK, that makes sense," Rita agreed. "But that doesn't explain why we keep acting out what we don't want, a marriage just like our parents had. I want that to stop!"

"Remember what I said?" I interjected. *"The marriage that you have right here and right now is the marriage you expect to have.* I didn't say that you **want** it, or that you **like** it. I didn't say that you **deliberately** made it happen. But I did say that it is what you expect to have. So you tell me, Neal, how will you have something different?"

"By having different expectations, right?"

"That's correct, Neal. *It's not too much more difficult than that*, really. Or better said, by diverting the expectations into the Marriage Blueprint that fits who you are here and now, you can build THAT marriage instead of the one you are currently building. **We are just going to use the knowledge, wisdom and experience you both have and turn the focus back to the marriage you wanted to build in the first place.**"

"How, Dr. Max? There is all this water under the bridge, all this pain and history. I don't know if I will be able to let go of all the bad things that have happened. You can't change the past."

"That's a common mistake that people make, Rita. You can change the past in some ways. True, you can't change events. But you can truly change your viewpoints about those events, your feelings, your mental picture of them. And you can totally change your response to them and how you use them in the future to manage your life together."

"Neal, can you think of something that happened to you as a kid that you saw one way then and now see very differently?"

"Sure. I had good athletic ability, but I didn't want to play sports. Mostly I hated practicing, because I found it boring. My father insisted that I play football and baseball, and attend every practice. I hated him for it at the time, but now I'm really glad I did it and followed through, and in the end I had a blast and got a scholarship. The things I did then in football and baseball, which helped me learn discipline and focus, have been really helpful for me later in life."

"That's a great example, Neal, and one I totally understand. I had a very similar deal with sports with my dad. Now let me drill this in, and I want you to see this very clearly. Ready?"

"Sure, put me in the game, coach!" Neal grinned. This time, Rita grinned too. Maybe she would start liking his sense of humor again.

"When you were playing sports, you were of two minds. On the one hand, you were furious at your Dad for forcing you to go to the practices and stay on the teams. But *on the other hand,* you started having success and pleasure, and another part of your mind was already beginning to view playing sports as a very positive thing, something you really wanted, and knew would make your life better, right?"

"Sure!"

"See how those two minds existed in one body? And even though one of them didn't go away, the one which didn't like being bullied by anyone..."

"He still has that mind—VERY active" Rita threw in.

"I sure do," Neal agreed. "I **hate** for people to tell me what to do."

"But you let your coaches, and now me, guide you, right?"

"That's different, Dr. Max."

"It's *absolutely* different, but you tell me why."

"Because I'm granting you permission."

"And you are doing that, why?"

"Because I am curious about what you are saying and you are making sense, so far anyway!" Again, that big, winning smile of Neal's. He sure didn't come into my office wearing it.

"And as I was saying, Neal, you had two sides at work within you, the side that never is going to like being pushed around, and the side that once you see something that makes sense to you, you are the very first person on board. *All I need to do with you is get you focused on the CORRECT Marriage Blueprint and you'll be right in the middle of building what you want and what's right for your family, I have a feeling.*"

"If Neal gets on board with something, he's an incredibly hard working and dedicated person. He's amazing," Rita said with a sparkle in her eye. "And a real genius also."

"Hey, Rita, thanks for saying that," Neal beamed. "But I've always seen you as the real creative thinker. Remember who designed our house, it wasn't me—it was your artistic vision."

"Hey, this is one of my favorite forms of competition between couples," I joined in. "I call it, *'You are more wonderful than I am, and I can prove it.'* You guys are cracking me up."

I could finally see the energy that had been there between them from their first meeting, the juice that drove their love from the beginning.

Now I knew exactly what my work was with this couple, and we could *go right for it.* I knew they would learn quickly and wouldn't need my help for very long at all. All I want to do in this book is show you these exact same things so you can be who you are and have a great marriage with the least trouble possible!

My view of therapy is the same as my view of parenthood: it should be there when you need it and go away when no longer needed —as soon as possible!

The work—your work too if you want to have a great marriage— is to understand how beliefs and your Marriage Blueprints determine the way you are married. The marriage you have right here and now is the marriage you expect to have!

### Want To Try Something Right Now?

- Write out all the beliefs you have about marriage—yours and other people's. What marriage is, what it does to people, how it changes their lives, the good, bad and ugly, what you learned from your parents, what you learned from your culture, what you learned from your friends who got married, what you've read and agreed with, what you read and disagreed with, everything.
- Then separate them into two columns, the ones you are living out right now (your here and now marriage) and the ones you aren't living out.

This is what Neal and Rita did. They discovered many things that amazed them about the beliefs, thoughts, feelings, attitudes and expectations that they had about marriage. They were shocked and stunned by all the beliefs they had which were driving them and which had resulted in them having exactly the opposite of the marriage they hoped for.

*Beliefs will do that.* **Beliefs drive everything, and whatever you are right now is the result of and the perfect reflection of those beliefs. This is no airy-fairy thing that you have to be into metaphysics to understand.** *Beliefs, just like bird-tracks, show in the sand.* **They show in everything you do, and make themselves obvious.**

You are going to see how certain beliefs you have which you actually thought you had "gotten over or aren't you" **are driving everything about your life.** Things you may not like at all—or alternatively things you like very much, but were afraid to act on.

No sweat. I'll just show you how to plug in some new ones, or do a better job of the ones you already have. Beliefs, as I'm using the term, are actually quite "plug n' play." **You can change the way you think and the results you get extremely rapidly.** No 5 years of go-nowhere therapy here.

Cold, hard reality—melted down by the intense flame of your desire and knowledge! *You are a welding torch just tearing through steel and softening it up to make it whatever you want it to be.*

If your marriage—or any other part of your life—is not going how you wish it were, and you aren't getting the results you want, I'm going to show you how you are getting exactly what you expect, and how to change the results you are getting.

But why would you believe me when I say this? I don't expect you to—I expect to *earn* that by hard work and talking with you—**and showing you what is inside of YOU, not inside of me—so that YOU can have a great marriage and great life.**

You may find that no matter what you say or do, you'll be touched by this book in positive ways and a seed will be sown that grows into *You Don't Have To Change Who You Are To Have a Great Marriage* inside of you, and you don't even have to work very hard at all to start seeing delicious fruit growing from that tree.

No matter what life you are living currently—I don't care where you are living or under what regime or in what kind of culture you are living—the things I'm telling you will help you get different, and better, results. It doesn't matter if you are black, white, red, green or chartreuse, old or young, male or female, straight or gay. The same principles work exactly the same way with every person.

Do yourself a favor and test it.

Hey, right now. Test this first chapter out for me. Aren't you **already** looking at your own marriage—and marriage in general—in a different way? **Don't you see already that powerful, positive changes can happen in your marriage, with much less effort, much less struggle and much less pain?**

Maybe you are already grasping deeply the message in the title of this book down deep in your body, soul and mind: *You Don't Have To Change Who You Are To Have A Great Marriage.* And maybe you haven't gotten it yet. You will or you won't. I don't know you that well. Let's test it out and see if it's true.

We've only just begun.

# CHAPTER TWO

## *The Intimacy Paradox* and How *You* Can Solve It
## (And Get What Everyone Wants But Few Really Get:
## True Intimacy)

*You Don't Have To Change Who You Are.* But **Who Are You?**

Ever feel like you have "multiple personalities" inside of you, or that maybe you are *"schizo?"*

With every important decision you make in your life, isn't there always something like a committee meeting going on inside your head? "Do this! No, do that! This is the best way! No, you'd be a fool, do it that way instead! Get married and have a baby! No, stay single! Go into this career, it's best for you! No, that one!"

Here's the "good news, bad news."

The good news is that if you have these internal conversations going on inside of you, you are *totally normal*, just like the rest of us.

The bad news is that if you don't get some good way of "organizing the committee" inside of you, you are going to go on—as most people do—feeling confused and unsure about whether you are making the right decisions.

Being unsure leads to something called "analysis paralysis." After a while, you just do what is comfortable and ultimately end up falling into ruts that you never intended to fall into.

Neal and Rita ended up living out their parents' marriages, despite their best intentions. Most of us as parents end up saying things to our children that are echoes of the exact things our own parents said—which we vowed we would never say or do.

Charlie, a young neighbor of mine said, "when I have kids, I'm going to really explain things to them and never tell them, 'It's because I said so, that's all. Just do it!' "

Good luck, Charlie.

Many of the things our families and cultures teach us are powerful and wonderful and we should definitely hang on to them and use them. But many things aren't.

A happy successful person has always resolved his family teachings and models with his own personal conclusions and discovered a "fit" which is his own personal style of acting, thinking, feeling and doing. We call this his "personality."

A happy successful person has a consistent personality style and it fits for who they are and want to be; they are the same on the inside as on the outside. They are whom they are both inside and out.

**Because of this consistency, the happy, successful person is able to choose well in life, because he knows what he wants and likes and what he wants to accomplish, and WHY he wants to do these things.**

Is it guaranteed he'll have a great marriage? Not necessarily, but he has a very good chance of it, especially after he has read this book. Everything I say will immediately make sense to this person.

An unhappy, unsuccessful person is blown by the winds around her and is confused. She (I'm going to go back and forth between "he" and "she" because this equally applies to men and women); she is influenced by everything around her because she has no strong, consistent sense of whom she is inside. So every good idea that comes along, she just "goes with it."

In the end she never knows who she is. And she ends up surprised that things happen to her that she never expected—and often what ends up happening to her is the exact opposite of what she wanted.

When you don't understand who you really are and what you really want, your "internal committee" will always be meeting, and you may experience emotional and spiritual conflict and confusion of what is "right" and what is "best."

**You don't want to be confused. You want to be clear.** It just works better.

When it comes to marriage, the best and happiest ones are the ones where:

- both people know who they are and what they want
- both people know who their partner is and what they want
- both people have 100% ability to keep their own integrity and feeling of their own individual personality
- both people have 100% acceptance of the other person's integrity and individual personality

---

### Dr. Max's "THE INTIMACY PARADOX"

**The Real Secret of ALL Great Marriages
Boils Down To Solving
The Intimacy Paradox**

**The Intimacy Paradox is this:
100% Acceptance of Yourself
PLUS
100% Acceptance of Your Spouse**

---

You must solve The Intimacy Paradox, if you are to have a Great Marriage! That's exactly what **you are going to solve by the end of this book!**

But you are going to have to keep your eye on the ball. This is going to go "fast and furious," and the changes happening inside of you, just like they were inside of Neal and Rita, may occur so fast you won't even notice.

Remember the old cowboy gunslinger joke about "I'm the fastest gun in the West. Want to see me draw my gun?" Then a split second later, when you've seen nothing at all, "Want to see it again?"

**That's how fast some of these changes are going to happen. You won't even know it until suddenly you wake up one morning and think, "I wonder how my marriage got so much better. I'm not doing anything different."**

You won't even remember how things got so much better in your marriage. And you won't even care how it happened.

# CHAPTER THREE

# You Are the World's Top Expert—on Your Marriage

"I pronounce You World's Greatest Instant Expert on Your Marriage."
—*Dr. Max*

Way to go!

Sometimes you get something called "unintended consequences." You do one thing and something quite different happens. A negative version of this is when you take a medicine for one symptom such as headache, and you end up with diarrhea. We call this a "side effect."

But sometimes you get something positive and wonderful that you didn't expect. That's called "serendipity."

This time you are going to get "serendipity!"

Even though you picked up a book on marriage, you are going to **know more about yourself as an individual person by the end of this book than you will reading any other book you have ever found.** It's because you will totally understand who you are, how you got to be who you are, and where you are going.

Your personality—your thoughts, feelings, attitudes, beliefs and actions—was put together step by step during your life. Who you are was constructed partly by your circumstances and partly by your own conclusions about those circumstances.

It was pretty systematic, this cobbling together of who you are. Far more systematic than you think. And all this means is that by making a few shifts in emphasis—not in your total personality, but just in a few things you do or think—you can get **totally different and more satisfying results.**

You'll deeply understand why you think, feel, imagine and act the way you do. Then you'll have the chance to make whatever kind of turn you want. Small shifts, medium changes or a total overhaul. It is up to you—and according to the kind of marriage you want to have.

You will stop the endless "committee meetings" going on in your head and clearly and decisively make decisions which move your life forward in the directions that YOU decide you want to go.

### A Brand New View of Marriages
### You Might Already Have a Great Marriage
### And Don't Even Know It

You have in your hands a revolutionary book.

Nothing like it has ever been written or even conceived of before.

You may very well discover you already have a far better marriage than you realize. Wouldn't that be a wonderful surprise?

You see, all other marriage books and courses have focused on what was "wrong" about your marriage. I am dedicated to showing you what is "right" about your marriage already and how you can take the wonderful wisdom, knowledge and skill you already have and use this wisdom to make sure that your life together can be everything you ever dreamed it could be!

It might sound a little corny, but I mean it very sincerely when I say that each of you is **already perfect deep down inside of you,** and there is something perfect and wonderful about you and your spouse already being together, maybe in this exact moment you don't see it, but many times others do.

### No Man-Bashing or Woman-Bashing

I'm not going to show you how one of you is wrong and one of you is right and how the "wrong" one needs to "straighten up his or her behavior."

Or that "if you only understood women" or "if you only understood men" your problems would disappear. That's just plain nonsense.

There's no man-bashing or woman-bashing in this book. (That alone makes it totally revolutionary!).

This is the only form of marriage therapy that truly includes and honors men in the process.

I'll tell you a lot more about that later.

The Marriage Blueprint System is all about finding your way to YOUR Great Marriage. It's about making you the **captain of your own ship,** the one you want to be on and the one you wish to steer—wherever you want to steer it.

There's no greater expert on you than you! There's no greater expert on what you truly want and believe in life than you! And there's no greater expert on your marriage than you!

My job is to show you in powerful, simple and efficient ways exactly how to get even more clarity on what you truly want and believe, and then how to bring those dreams into your life more quickly and more dramatically than you can even imagine.

### Miracles? Serve Mine With Meat and Potatoes Please!

Do you believe in miracles? I don't mean the kind where Moses parts the Red Sea or the mountain moves to Mohammed. I mean the kind where extraordinary and powerful changes toward abundance, wealth and happiness come to ordinary people like us?

If you do believe in miracles like this, you are in for a treat. I'm going to show you exactly how to make them come your way by simply changing the way you go about getting the things you truly want in life.

Amazingly, a lot of it has to do with something very simple, which is *settling down and understanding that who you are is already good enough.*

If you don't believe in miracles like this, don't worry. You don't have to. Just think of it this way: Whether **you believe or not, if dramatic and desired changes come in your life, who cares how they get there?**

Something I do better than just about anyone else is to help people get those kinds of miraculous changes in their marriages. I've been doing this with folks for 25 years, and now you get the distilled power and practical tools that come from all that work.

Half of the time, even I am stunned at the kinds of incredible changes that can happen in people's lives when they get this revolutionary understanding and knowledge, and the ease with which it can happen.

All you need to do is to stop focusing on the idea that something is wrong or bad or a problem, and start focusing on the idea that something is right and good and a solution, and a lot of things can happen really quickly and powerfully in your life.

- It's important so that you understand **why** you get angry, frustrated, hurt, betrayed and insulted by other people.
- It's important so that you recognize the source of that hurt—and can see that the *source of that hurt is really not in the other person,* but in your own beliefs and expectations of the other person.
- It's important so that you can be free of the traps you have gotten into in your marriage or long term relationships when you end up feeling confused and frustrated and saying things like "I thought I knew him/her" and "I never saw this coming."
- I'll show you exactly why this happens to you and what to do about it so you can be free of these kinds of emotional and mental traps.

We believe in freedom, and yet *emotionally and mentally most people are not free, but living in the tyranny of their thoughts and feelings.* I want you to be free! And I want to show you a powerful, effective and very simple way to be free in the shortest time possible.

### How LONG will it take?
### I Want Changes NOW.
### OK, That Can Happen!

People usually ask, "How long will therapy take?" My answer is always, "Five minutes! But your **getting ready** for those five minutes might take a while, because you might have to fight change and transformation for a long time. **It's entirely up to you how long it is before your five minutes of total transformation occur.**"

That's not a light statement. Some things really do have to happen to make you ready for those "five minutes" in your marriage. One of them is that you have to stop thinking about things the way you are now, and start seeing everything from a new angle.

New angles from which you will see marriage in general and your marriage will shock and delight you. Then when you see how easy it is to change I think you'll just get a smile on your face and say, "I kind of knew that all along!"

### At The End of This Book,
### I Hope You Grin and Say
### "I Knew That Already!"

That's the nature of genuine revolutions or big changes in life. When they start, everyone thinks they are a little crazy and different. Once things truly start to change, it feels natural, right, and you can't imagine you once did things any other way.

When you understand "how the marriage in your mind determines the marriage in your heart, and how to have the life together you always dreamed of"—and start living by this way of thinking and believing—it will feel so natural and surprising you might even forget that things were any other way.

You'll get it why some marriages seem to be wonderful and fantastic and the people in them so happy, even though it seems like they "do everything wrong," and why some marriages seem to just never work, even though people "do everything right."

This time you are truly in the right place at the right time.

### We are ALL in this Together!

And let me say for the record that I believe this work will help you tremendously in your relationships and marriages no matter what your sexual orientation. As human beings we are all subject to the same laws and effects of Belief System creation and live together within the same world of influences; our minds all work similarly.

# CHAPTER FOUR

## Tom and Sandy—
## Why "Being Perfect"
## Won't Bring You Marital Happiness

Welcome back, Instant Expert!

Well, *not a full fledged expert yet,* but you are well on your way to unlocking the secret code behind happy marriages which you will easily use to have your own success, and which you can use to help others you know who might be suffering, too.

Just think if you *showed two friends* how they can have a great marriage with only a little increased understanding and compassion, wouldn't that be a wonderful thing? It's great to help yourself and even greater to help other people, wouldn't you agree?

Let me tell you about two couples I know: Tom and Sandy, and Rick and Donna.

**The CODE for great marriages is in these two stories.** When you read these two stories and think about your own marriage (and your friends', too) you'll quickly understand why some marriages "go wonderful from the get-go" and others are doomed from the first day.

Don't get hung up on the circumstances of their marriages, but try to see the point. It's like one of those famous movies about boxers. You might not even like boxing but you can see that the movie is about coming from behind and being a strong, determined underdog and winning despite the odds. It's not about boxing at all.

What you'll understand is that it's *not circumstances* that determine great marriages, but something new we've discovered, something that you've never heard before—the Marriage Blueprint.

Be thinking: Which marriage story reminds you most of your own?

## Tom and Sandy

Tom and Sandy look like the *perfect couple.* They have the "right life," and seem to do "everything right." **Yet it seems that it comes out wrong,** no matter what they do.

They too have been married 19 years. They have a house that, while not a villa on the Riviera, is definitely *upscale.* Tom has done *extremely* well with his company, and Sandy, although only working part-time, is one of the top property listers with her real estate brokerage.

Neither one has ever had an extramarital affair, although they both confess to having "been tempted."

Money is "not a problem." They have been quite fortunate.

They both describe their sex life as "fantastic," although they admit that in recent years the "flame seemed to have died a bit," but they both think maybe this just has to do with aging.

Tom and Sandy both have a great sense of humor and can usually find something funny about anything.

They are smart and quick and easily entertain each other with their wit. Both being well read and as Sandy says, "totally overeducated," they are real students of history, economics and politics. When they travel together for fun they have very similar interests in exploring both the fun parts of the places they visit as well as the points of historical interest.

To be with them is to be around a couple who seem so perfectly skillful, beautiful, fun-loving and socially adept as to appear like the ideal couple and to have the marriage everyone might want to have.

### "Perfect Children"

Tom and Sandy have two sons who have excelled in high school and are constantly receiving awards for their excellence in each of their interests.

They both love golf, boating, fine dining, and being involved with their family. Tom serves on the board the local hospital, and Sandy is a very active volunteer with the Red Cross. They describe their life as "almost perfect, with a few exceptions." But those "exceptions" certainly take their toll.

## "The Only Problems"

There were only two things that Sandy named as "problems" in their marriage.

First, that Tom occasionally went on drinking binges for a whole weekend (when she would not know where he was).

And second, that he was always planning an extended trip with his buddies to far away golfing locations around the world. On these trips he would spend a lot of money , be away from the family for a couple of weeks at a time, turn off his cell phone and refuse to give her a telephone number.

In fact, he only goes on these trips about once every six months or so, and in the last year only once. But when it happens the fallout from it can be intense.

And when he returned from these trips, he would be completely tight lipped about exactly where he had been and what all he had done. He would get a stern look on his face when asked about it and would say, "Golf! That's what I do on my golf trips, play golf! Why do you have to question me?"

Instantly, Sandy feels hurt, betrayed and abandoned by Tom's actions and responses. In her view, she's never questioned him about his love for the sport or his involvement in it, nor even really that he plans these trips.

## "Sandy Feels Completely Shut Out!"

It's more that she feels completely shut out, dismissed and insulted by his treatment of her when she "only asks the basic information" about where he is and how to get hold of him.

Sandy said, "I know it sounds absolutely horrible, but at these times I honestly just hate him and wish he would just die on his trip!"

At times, despite the satisfaction of the rest of their life together, Sandy has *seriously considered divorcing Tom* (a thought which always surprises even her). She says that the pain of these occasional events is so extreme, so unnerving and provoking so much anxiety in her that she sometimes thinks that she may have married the wrong man, or that she should get out now while she is still young, and try to find someone more compatible with her.

With every one of these incidents, or even **mention** of them, Sandy feels as if her whole life is falling apart, and every time she feels less like she can trust Tom at all!

His "disappearances," as Sandy calls them, create such anxiety first in her and then in him, that their whole life gets disrupted. When he comes home from these trips or from a weekend binge, they both dread the outcome of it.

## "The Silent Treatment"

These actions set off days or even more than a week of "The Silent Treatment" between them, when they barely speak to one another. Both feel hurt and each feel resolved inside that "I'm not going to be the one to make up—I didn't do anything wrong so why should it be up to me to straighten this out?"

In a few days or sometimes a week or so, the hurt seemed to dissipate and they would be back to talking, sleeping together and "back to our life together."

They both describe these "Silent Treatment" times as painful, confusing and a waste of time. Yet they both feel quite justified in their positions and see nothing wrong with what they are thinking and feeling about the conflict and their own views of what is right and wrong—and they can't see a way around this complete difference of opinion.

When it's happening they don't even **want** to find a way to resolve it!

Tom: "Sandy's Incredibly Needy and Clingy"

Tom says that the "only problem" between him and Sandy is that she can get "incredibly needy and clingy" and that this always surprises him since he views her as an accomplished and very independent person in her own right. *He says he "can't stand her" when she "gets clingy like that,"* and in those moments he too feels like he might have just chosen the wrong person to be married to. He describes the feeling he gets toward her as "feeling nauseated and just sick all over!"

Their oldest son, Jack, graduates from high school this year, and will be following a successful high school experience with a half scholarship to one of the best State schools. He was recruited both on the basis of excellence in sports and strong academic ability.

Younger son Bob is a freshman and has unmistakable gifts as an artist. Tom himself had demonstrated similar gifts as a high school student, and had always regretted that he never followed through with his artistic talents.

Tom and Sandy are very proud of their children, and feel great about their parenting. However, recently they have begun to have some slight doubts.

### "Trouble In Paradise"

Just recently Jack was stopped by the local police for reckless driving. He had been drinking heavily with his friends. He got a DUI, and his license has been revoked.

Tom found out that in fact Jack had been lucky to only get a DUI, since he and his friends had a substantial stash of other drugs in the car that night. The policeman told Jack in private that he was going to let the drug situation go, since he knew the family and was certain that this was only an isolated incidence.

Jack told his father about this and Tom made it clear that this part of the deal was to be "their little secret" and that Jack was under no circumstances to tell his mother about the drugs, because "she would go ballistic." More "Silent Treatment!"

### "Jack's Defiance"

Jack was surprisingly defiant about the whole situation and said that he "had worked hard all the way through school and had a right to have fun and get drunk in his senior year."

Jack had a steady girlfriend, Amy, who got furious with him when she found out about the trouble. She told him that if that's the kind of guy he was, she had no interest in dating him anymore. Jack told her in no uncertain terms that he didn't feel like being put in a straight-jacket by "any woman."

Tom actually kind of chuckled to himself inside and thought, "he's a chip off the old block!"

### "Bob's Irritable Bowel Syndrome"

About the same time, younger son Bob had a very strong episode of asthma and also began having symptoms of Irritable Bowel Syndrome.

Their family physician prescribed some medications and said that he was very concerned about Bob and the whole family also, and that they should consider counseling or family therapy. He said that Bob's diagnosis was "not physical but mental. He's like a person under tremendous stress, like some of the executives I see who are 3 times his age."

They subsequently (in their words) "burned through six different therapists," spending thousands and thousands of dollars, hours, time and energy, and in the end they had this to say about it:

"We learned lots of great tools, and left the therapy sessions every time with a feeling of hopefulness that we would be able to resolve this basic conflict. But in the end nothing really changed. It's just the same as it was before!"

### "Things Are Falling Apart. What Would You Advise?"

Now as you read this, you might think you have some kind of answer. And if you were the therapist or counselor consulted in this case (or were Tom and Sandy's friend), then it might seem clear to you what should happen.

I'm sure you would have some advice for them.

I'll bet you think you know exactly what needs to happen here.

If you do, then you are right in there with the majority of therapists.

*And if you do, then you probably are going to make the exact same mistakes with this family that 99% of all marriage therapists and counselors make with couples.*

And you are going to fail in helping this couple, like the vast majority of couples therapy indeed does.

### Tom and Sandy, Happy Ending

I'm happy to tell you that Tom and Sandy were able to find a very creative and satisfying solution to their stand-off. They were both able to feel respected, understood and loved. According to Sandy, "our marriage is the best it's ever been—and we never thought it was bad." They are planning what they call a "re-dedication ceremony," where they plan to renew their vows, as Tom says "on a whole different level. We've finally discovered what true intimacy is!"

Knowing Tom and Sandy, I can guarantee you it will be quite a shindig. They are going all out, and the last I heard Tom is inviting a famous singer they both love to play at the ceremony.

What they found that made the difference to them is what you will discover in this book, and especially in Part III—the Marriage Blueprints! With the information I gave them about beliefs and models of marriages and families, many of these seemingly unsolvable differences have become almost effortless to resolve.

If you have been to marriage therapy or counseling before, you know how "draggy" and tiresome the process can be. Not at all with my methods! You'll be surprised how quickly and how permanently you can get change with my models. It's enjoyable, and you can do it yourself.

**Very little traditional marriage and family therapy has sticking power.** Sure, lots of "standard" advice and therapy can put a band-aid on the situation and make it better for a little while. Just about everyone can come up with good advice that will temporarily make the situation much better.

And many therapists and other people believe that by having the couple and family discuss their differences and points of view, there is a very good chance that they will come to some kind of understanding which will help them get past these conflicts and resolve them.

Unfortunately, that's not the case.

## True, Sometimes You Have To Start With Just Plain Better Behavior

Many times good advice (including religious instruction) can help people in marriages. I'm not knocking it—at all. As a matter of fact, I have a book for that called *Ten Days to a Good Marriage: Turn Your Marriage Around in Ten Days or Less*. You can find it at www.TenDaysToAGoodMarriage.com

The focus of "Ten Days to a Good Marriage" and this kind of relationship advice is to get behavior up to a *"workable minimum standard."* Many times people are behaving so badly that nothing they try to do will work, because the first thing that needs to happen is better behavior! It's like when your kids are acting up—you have to get their attention to give them guidance—and that means you have to interrupt their current behavior and get them to straighten up first, before you can do anything else with them.

Oftentimes, helping people with their communication skills with one another (such as active listening or empathic listening or a million other methods) will help.

The problem is that for many couples such as Tom and Sandy, even the best therapist techniques that have been developed (up until now!) will only help in a very limited way—and for conflicts which are not really very deep seated or critical.

*In other words, advice and therapy up to this point have only been effective in cases when they were not absolutely essential!*

A lot of couples can benefit from traditional therapy, and even from basic theory models about human beings, such as Christian counseling, feminist counseling, psychic consultations, Myers-Briggs testing or behavior modification.

If a couple is already "basically in the zone" with their marriage, but they have gotten a little off course, the truth is that almost any kind of therapy or counseling will help.

The fact is not a very happy one nor is it often discussed among therapists, but different methods of therapy don't really differ much in their results. It's mostly a matter of the fact that the couple has decided to address an issue that is the helpful ingredient. In other words, most couples therapy (in fact, most therapy in general) could easily be considered "placebo."

And that doesn't even matter much, if you think about it. If the couple that basically has a good relationship feels that the communication methods or advice they get from whatever source helps them, then God bless them!

## But There's A World of Effective, Powerful Change WAY Beyond "Good Advice!"

However, what I've found over the years is that none of the traditional models of marriage therapy seem to truly help in the long run if there are really deep seated differences that "won't go away" with the use of techniques—no matter how well thought out they are!

Sure, people may stay together.

They might say they are staying together "for the kids," "because I don't believe in divorce," "because I think people should keep their promises," or because of many other reasons.

I'm not criticizing those reasons.

But I am saying these two things:

1. It might be very possible to stay together and be extremely happy and fulfilled and joyful doing so.
2. Traditional models of therapy, religious or "theory" based models of marriage and marriage counseling may **never help you** with the part about staying together that includes "being extremely happy and fulfilled and joyful doing so."

If a couple is exhorted by their religious community—or by their friends or by some relationship expert—to stay together, they might very well go ahead and stay together.

## You Don't Have To Change
## Who You Are
## To Have a Great Marriage

If you are going to stay together, shouldn't it be possible to also be extremely fulfilled and joyful about it to, and not in some "fake" or "imposed" way, but really, truly and genuinely from the inside out, and never feeling that you have to compromise your true self to do so?

Most of the models of "stay-together-no-matter-what" include the command to compromise what feels most true to you and your basic character to do so.

**That stinks!** And it's totally unnecessary.

You might say you feel good "doing the right thing by staying together," but if you are doing that and compromising who you really are and what you really think, feel and believe about yourself, we both know you are living a lie and that you are strangling your soul!

- Let's find a way that your soul, your mind, your feelings and your imagination can be freed.
- Let's find a way that the true *power, majesty and holy meaning* of marriage can be genuinely experienced and expressed between you and your partner.
- Let's find a way that the power of being together in marriage and the holy sacrament of marriage can be **combined with the**

**joy** of being a unique human being—where your own thoughts, feelings and views about yourself can be combined!

Being married doesn't mean that you can't be an individual, and being an individual doesn't mean that you can't be married.

Sometimes people get confused about that.

But before we go headlong into this topic of how you can truly be yourself in your marriage, let me tell you about another, very different couple.

# CHAPTER FIVE

## Rick and Donna—Flawed But Happy:
## The Code for Your Great Marriage
## (They Solved the Code. And If They Did, You Can Too!)

### *Rick and Donna*

When Mose Allison sings, "I just want to do everything wrong and still pick up first prize," I think of the following couple.

Rick and Donna, viewed by Hollywood or "upper crust" standards, are not likely to win "beautiful couple of the year award."

In Rick's words, "We ain't perfect." ☺

They've had some *real struggles* in their 24 years of married life—especially in the world of their finances. One of their jokes together is "there's no financial problem that can't be solved by getting a larger loan."

Rick is a very skilled carpenter and mason. Donna loves to say about him, "Rick can build anything, faster and better than anyone on the planet. He's a genius." Unfortunately, he's *not* a genius when it comes to finances, nor is Donna.

A few years ago, Rick decided to take a step up to having his own contracting business, partly because he began to have a lot of work related injuries that just compounded and compounded, and he was afraid of becoming permanently laid up.

Rick refused to go to the doctor, because he says "they are all crooks and don't know anything I can't figure out on my own."

He got swindled on three business deals in a row and they lost almost all their savings—barely avoided losing their home. Donna says about this, "I'm dumb about business dealings, but Rick is even dumber. I think it's because he'll give away the shirt on his back if he thinks it will make someone feel better—he's all heart."

Rick says that the compliment is a bit lost on him, and that Donna digs him about it on an almost daily basis. He grins when he says this.

Donna constantly struggles with her weight, and is constantly on a diet (and constantly breaking it). She has tried numerous jobs, but in the end gets frustrated with someone at work and walks out.

They both have lifelong friends as individuals and long time friends as a couple. Many of the couples they know have broken up, gotten remarried, or even remarried to the same partner after a divorce.

## Rick: "We Just Talk Our Problems Out What's so Hard About That?"

Donna and Rick say the same thing about this: "We don't understand what's so hard about marriage or about solving problems, you just talk them out! What's so hard about that?"

They have a daughter and a son. The daughter Teva is 22 and had a child by an unknown father two years ago. She is living with Rick and Donna "until I get it together." Donna loves that granddaughter, and although they tell Teva every day that she's "got to get her sh%% together and go make it on her own," it's clear that Donna loves that grandkid and talks about the child all the time.

Their son Paul (14 years old) is a quiet kid and plays on the computer a lot. He's got some very good friends with whom he plays computer games and listens to music. At best a "C" student, he is not sure what he'll do after high school. For now, he really enjoys his games and always looks forward to the frequent family camping trips because he loves fishing (a boy after my own heart!).

### Paul is Amused By His Parents

Paul says he loves these camping trips even though his parents tend to get a bit drunk and loud and tell too many of the same stories again and again. He thinks they are idiots, but he *says so with a smile* and confesses he'd never want to miss any of these camping trips, and that he always stays up with them and their friends into the night around the campfire.

Rick and Donna always seem to be in a fight of some kind. They have big disagreements on almost every topic that comes up—parenting, sex, politics, religion, money, you name it and they fight about it.

If you are around them you know it's likely to be loud and intense.

## "They Break All the Rules"

They "break all the rules" of communication that have been laid down by experts in counseling and psychology. They blame each other, they don't really listen to each other, they hold on to grudges and dig each other about it. They bring up the past and rub it in. They bring their kids into the arguments and try to get the kids to take sides. They undermine each other on the discipline of the kids. They sneakily spend money behind the other's back.

Their sex life is no great shakes either (to use a pun). Because of pain medication and blood pressure medicine that Rick takes, he is sometimes impotent. But he's found modern erectile dysfunction drugs work just fine. Donna is a little embarrassed by her body size, and sometimes says that thinking about this can get in the way of enjoying sex. Although she confesses a little coyly, "When I do have an orgasm, it will usually be like how I am most of the time anyway—loud, big and intense—really fun!"

In other words, it would be easy to say that they "do everything wrong in their marriage, *by the book.*"

## "But It Comes Out Right"

But, funny thing is, it seems that despite the fact that they "do everything wrong," it seems to always "come out right."

They both insist they would never be with anyone else, and that they can only imagine growing old (and fussing and fighting) right up to their last breath—and beyond the grave, if possible.

Whether you talk to Rick or Donna alone or together, you get the same answers about their marriage. "We belong together, we have a great marriage through thick and thin." Neither one ever even thinks about getting divorced, no matter what the problems are that occur in life.

Their view? "Problems come along in life no matter what. It's just much better to have someone there to work through them with. We love each other and would never even think about breaking up."

Donna actually had a brief affair years ago, which Rick knows about. He says it bugs him, but he says he had to "get over it" because "people mess up, but that's no reason you should have to get rid of them." He says, "It could have just as easily been me." That's not to say he doesn't bring the topic up now and then to "get Donna's goat."

Ultimately though, I can't imagine anything that could drive Rick and Donna apart, even though they have "no end" of problems.

They seem to do "everything wrong" and yet it always turns out right for them.

They have a Great Marriage.

### "Why is it a great marriage?
### You know the answers"

Do you know why? Can you explain why and how they do have this great relationship?

Most experts would have a hard time explaining it.

Experts might try to explain it on the basis of something like "pheromones" or basic hormonal compatibility. They might try to find some social factors such as friends, family or activities that drive their loyalty to one another.

But these "reasons" will completely miss the point.

Do you know why their relationship is so solid, long lasting and satisfying to them despite all these factors that might seem to drive a wedge into many marriages?

### "You *Don't* Have To Have the *Perfect Family* or Know Anything More Than You Already Do to Have a Great Marriage. It Takes Far Less Than You Think"

If you DO know why Rick and Donna's marriage is a great one, you are very much ahead of the researchers in my field (except me, of course :) and most clinicians.

I'll bet you do know. It's kind of common sense on steroids!

This marriage really doesn't fit the model by any stretch of the imagination of the "ideal" or "model" couple.

Is your marriage like either Tom and Sandy's, or Rick and Donna's?

Remember, I don't mean their circumstances, but how they truly relate to one another.

Were you able to identify with either one of these relationships? What makes your marriage feel "great" or "awful?"

---

*The puzzling questions for a long time now in marriage therapy are these:*

- *Why do some couples seem to have great marriages **no matter what they do**—and why do other couples seem to have bad or extremely painful marriages **no matter what they do?***

- *Why is it that with some couples a **few simple techniques** (or methods, instruction, advice or skills) seem to get the marriage really on track—and with other couples, no amount of skill, focus, methods, advice or help seem to work at all?*

- *Why do some couples **immediately get how to use help from others and immediately make changes** in their marriage and get incredible satisfaction from just a little help?*

- *And other couples seem to never "grasp" or be able to use anything we do with them?*

*What I'm showing you is how to have a **Great Marriage**. But I don't want you to confuse a Great Marriage with one that lasts a long time.*

---

### Long Term Marriage is Not Necessarily Praiseworthy!

**Great Marriages often do last a long time. But so do a lot of mediocre and unsatisfying marriages.**

A lot of people stick together for a very long time, and are completely miserable. Is that an achievement? Well, I guess, if you consider suffering for a very long time something praiseworthy. Like those Indian Gurus who lie down on "beds of nails" and somehow endure the pain, or the guys who eat glass. I don't know about you, but I can't see the point of voluntary suffering! There's enough suffering we encounter in life that I can't support someone accepting or volunteering for it. You might disagree with me, and you might even like suffering.

Remember the joke about the sadist (one who enjoys inflicting pain) and the masochist (one who enjoys pain). The masochist says, "beat me, beat me!" The sadist grins and says, "No!"

Would you like to have a marriage that can last a long time AND that can be deeply satisfying and full of joy and meaning?

Here's what I ruled out—and you need to rule these out too, or you will constantly be going down the wrong road in trying to have a great marriage.

### Great marriages *DON'T* depend on:

- Having financial security or high income
- Having a shared religious background or belief
- Knowing and using the right communication methods
- Going to therapy
- Having shared interests
- Having the same SPOKEN values about marriage and family
- Having great sex
- Having children
- Having rewarding careers
- Having passionate personal interests
- Being young and beautiful
- "Fighting Fair"
- Having a high level of personal spiritual development
- Educational background

Don't get me wrong.

I'm not saying that these things are bad. I'm not saying you shouldn't have these things. I'm not saying that these things won't necessarily help you be happy in your marriage.

What I've discovered though is that these things (and I especially want to emphasize religious commitment) do not produce Great Marriages.

### If Great Marriage is the itch,
### These things do not really scratch the itch.

They scratch "around" the itch, but they never hit it.

You know when you want someone to scratch your back, and you say, a little higher, a little lower, to the right, to the left.

If they don't hit the itch, what happens?

You start itching all over, right?

If they do hit the itch, doesn't it provide immediate relief?

What I'm giving you is a scratch that truly hits the itch.

**What DOES matter in creating your Great Marriage?** If all these things that we usually think of as helping to create a great marriage don't do the job, what does?

## What matters is something I call
## Your Marriage Blueprint™

You know what a blueprint is.

A blueprint is the name given to an illustration describing the structural plan, usually for a building or other construction plan.

It is a set of plans that represents the final structure in schematic design.

It's a drawing with specific instructions of an image.

A person has a view of a house they would like to build, either in their own mind as an original image or more often as an influenced combination of images of houses they have seen in the past along with their personal touch.

First, there's the image that you start with of a house or other building. Then there's a drawing that a draftsman makes of that image (as close as he or she can be to the image you have in your head, given the possibilities and laws of physics and your county's building code). This drawing includes what needs to be done and in what way that image in your head can be translated into a real house you can walk into and live in.

Once the draftsman draws the blueprint of the house, you hand it to the contractor who figures out what materials, processes, workers and sequences are necessary to make a drawing of your house into your real house.

Very few people would ever set about building a house without a good set of blueprints describing in detail the needed materials, dimensions, fittings and joinery that is necessary to build that house.

In most places in the industrialized world, it's actually illegal to build a house without a blueprint and corresponding permits being issued by your place of residence that assures safety and soundness of your house.

Permits are issued by counties and other municipalities that are meant to provide public safety and your own personal safety. Engineers have carefully studied ratios and spans and materials in order to provide minimal standards to withstand certain levels of wind, earth tremors, snow and weight, and reduced these to design and materials requirements.

We conform to these requirements because we have to, but also because we recognize the need to grant respect to those who understand such engineering specifics. We want our house to last a long time, be stable, strong and secure, as well as pleasing and useful to us.

It's ironic in some ways that we've been so careful and thoughtful about requiring people to have and produce blueprints of the kinds of buildings they want to build, and get permits, and yet what is even more important, marriage, requires no blueprints at all.

No one would start building a modern, wired, plumbed, electrical and/or gas-powered house without a detailed plan of some kind.

**Yet most people will start building relationships and marriages without the slightest thought that they need a blueprint or plan to be successful in marriage!**

The vast majority of people just go headlong into marriage hoping eventually it will be OK or that they will figure it out along the way.

**What few people realize is that they have active blueprints or models of marriage and relationship already working in the background unconsciously driving their thoughts, feelings and actions in marriage—and those models are often in conflict inside of them or in conflict with their new partner's blueprint of what a marriage should be.**

These blueprints—the 8 most common patterns—will be the subject of part III, the most revolutionary part of this book! You'll see your best vision of marriage portrayed in them, and also why many times you and your partner deeply disagree on some of the important issues of parenting, such as money, sex and parenting.

# CHAPTER SIX

## How To Be Bold in Marriage—Or *Even in Divorce!*

A revolutionary concept: **no one can tell you what a Great Marriage is!** You have to find out for yourself. I don't care how great or wonderful your therapist, guru, pastor, counselor or television personality is. They don't know the answer! I don't know the answer. All I can do is show you how to find the answer for yourself!

The most important reason is for you to see that there is absolutely nothing wrong, and everything right about what you want to have in your own marriage.

You have the wisdom to know what you desire!

There's not just one single *Hollywood version of marriage,* and there is certainly no religion or cult on earth that has the right to say, "We have the right, single and perfect answer."

### The Next Step:
### Focus ON SOLUTIONS, not problems!
### If you focus on problems, you'll get problems
### If you focus on solutions, you'll get solutions

I recognized that the usual advice and counseling about marriage and long term relationships was sorely lacking. In the marriages where the greatest help was needed—where marriages were under very severe threat of divorce—the usual counseling both from traditional and religious models just didn't get to the core.

**Anything that focuses on problems is going to get stuck on problems. If you focus on solutions, you'll get solutions!**

Of course, very few couples come to therapy when they should. They almost always wait until it is either too late, or almost too late, to make a comeback or start over with the marriage. Usually, the point of coming to therapy is at the absolute breaking point.

If you are beginning to experience conflict in your marriage or have already gotten right up to the threshold of divorce or dissolution, you will have a brand new set of tools and understanding that goes to the real core of the conflicts, and why they are there in the first place. **And you will be able to understand what truly needs to be straightened out in your *head* for your *heart* to be married.**

- You must have a **quick,** powerful understanding of the deep, true and real source of your differences and conflict
- You need to know what to do and why **right away** (not after a year or two of weekly sessions)

Years of intense observation have produced the key, which is working with **your** Marriage Blueprint. You now will have that key.

When you have this key, you'll solve some puzzles.

- You'll know why thoughts, feelings and actions that you have sometimes work wonderfully in your marriage.
- You'll know why thoughts, feelings and actions you have sometimes don't work at all in your marriage.
- You'll know why some marriages *effortlessly succeed,* and how you can draw on the wealth of wisdom that they have in them (without even trying).
- You'll know why some marriages *never really succeed* and why that happens.

And then, even more importantly:

- You'll be able to know what kinds of actions will succeed in helping you have an extremely satisfying and joyous marriage.
- You'll be able to know what kinds of actions will NOT succeed in helping you have an extremely satisfying and joyous marriage.

**If you decide to stay in your marriage,** you'll know exactly why and what to do to make that marriage satisfying for you and your partner.

Alternatively, if you decide to end your marriage, you'll know exactly why and will not have to carry the guilt and sense of failure that so many people have when they end a marriage.

---

### A note about divorce and separation (very important)

#### Divorce is JUST CHANGE
*It's a natural part of a long life for many people.*

#### DIVORCE IS NOT FAILURE!
#### DO NOT FEEL ASHAMED IF YOU
#### HAVE BEEN DIVORCED

*Most people feel like they have failed*
*if their marriage ends in divorce*
*That's* **CRAP**

---

Some people disagree with me.

"You are supporting divorce and encouraging people to get divorced, which is awful and horrible!" This is a common statement. Wrong. I don't think divorce is a casual choice or one which one should take easily or without thinking about it carefully. It's a rough road. But the fact is that everyone in the modern world is directly affected by divorce and it's time we see it for what it is: just another part of human change that's here to stay. It's not going to go away.

### The divorce rate in the United States is 100%

How can I say that? I say that because not one single person in the United States is *untouched* by divorce.

Every single person is either divorced, will be divorced, has a relative or parents who divorced, friends who divorced, parents of friends who divorced, classmates who divorced, classmates whose parents are divorced, or other acquaintances who have gone through divorce. You get the point.

Divorce touches every single person in the United States, and it's just a fact of our lives.

Do I like it? No. Do I think it's funny? No.

But I think it is real. And I want you to face it head on and understand it, just like I'm asking you to do with every other part of your married life.

The fact is that you have the option to get divorced any time you like.

You might think that is sad or wrong, but it's totally true.

And recognize that one of the most powerful decisions you can make, or will ever make, will come out of freedom and knowledge that you have.

Some people feel that divorce "is not an option," because they have a religious view about marriage or because they "made a promise" or because they are afraid it says something negative about them as a human being. I understand that.

However, just as many people with these "it's-not-an-option" positions get divorced as everyone else.

I'd much rather you have a Great Marriage! Far prefer that! But what I'm saying is that part of having a Great Marriage is having the knowledge and freedom to choose a Great Marriage.

This power comes from having the truth in front of you. Here's more truth.

Let's put it bluntly: It's ridiculous to say that marriages that end in divorce imply failure on your part.

People live a long time these days. In those many years we live, each and every one of us continues to grow, develop and change. Frequently our tastes change. Look at your high school yearbook picture and look at yourself in the mirror now. Any changes?

Of course there are.

Did you learn new things in any area over the last years, say about life, money, sex, politics, business, friendship, parenting, any interests you might have, that now influence your views of life very differently than when you were 18 years old.

Is it clear that individuals change?

Is it clear that you have changed?

So tell me this, how likely is it that two individuals, just because they have been married for twenty years, will have stayed the same as they were at 20 years old, or alternatively that they will have changed in exactly the same ways that are 100% compatible over the period of 20 years?

Very low, isn't it?

Then why should you be ashamed?

Sometimes people change enough that it makes no sense to stay together. And sometimes their views on marriage are in such drastic contrast that it creates a lot of friction.

Sometimes this contrast is fine. Sometimes it is too much (for you, because it is UP TO YOU to decide), and you just don't want to do it anymore.

### Divorce is no shame

**I'm not advocating divorce.** And I'm not advocating NO divorce! What I am advocating is that *it is up to you and no one else.* It's nobody else's business what you do.

But whatever you decide, be happy about it and make it a conscious and deliberate choice. Just don't try to knock your mind out of it and act like you don't have any choice.

If you are going to be married, be married boldly and work it out. Do the things you ought to do and create a Great Marriage.

If you are going to get divorced, get divorced and make it a good, successful and happy divorce. Go to www.CouplesCoach.com , where along with all of the information about how to have a good or great marriage, there is information and help for having a good divorce. Recent and valuable research is available there which will help you understand how to have a very positive divorce, if that's where you are headed.

Having a good divorce is not that hard, if you get your mind set on it and get some good advice. Many of the commonly held ideas about divorce have not held up or are just "old wives' tales."

Just don't be a whiner whatever you choose to do. Be alive and keep your eye on the ball. Be in the game.

Here's what I'm saying:

> *If you are going to be married, be married boldly, joyfully, and with honesty and courage. If you are going to get divorced, get divorced boldly, joyfully, and with honesty and courage.*
>
> *Whatever you do, do it with boldness and courage.*

## Your Two Views of Marriage
### Let's Go Boldly Where Others Have Not Dared to Tread

Now, we haven't identified your Marriage Blueprint yet, but I can tell you now that you have two basic Marriage Blueprints: The one you developed as a child, which I call your *Family Marriage Blueprint*. And the one you layered over that as an adult, which I call your *Personal Marriage Blueprint*.

If you look carefully, you'll see both. What you grew up believing, seeing, observing and "receiving" from "the environment" (that is, your parents, other relatives, neighbors) is the first: the Family Marriage Blueprint.

And then there is something you worked on more deliberately later in childhood and on into adulthood, which didn't automatically imprint on you, but rather you DECIDED was the way you want to live. This is your Personal Marriage Blueprint.

These two are frequently in conflict (but NOT ALWAYS!).

They call for very different "Marriage Houses" to be built.

They usually don't match.

And they always drive your thoughts, feelings and actions in your life in Marriage. Often the differences between them can "drive you to distraction!"

### Marriage Gets Complicated For Most of Us

For most of us, marriage and the intimacy paradox is going to get a little complicated to solve before it becomes easy. If you've been married over a year, you already know this. Marriage, like everything, has certain codes—which if you know them, you make it work. And if you don't, well, you drown.

Most of us are constantly changing our loyalties. At one time we like one thing, then soon after we like something quite different. We are swayed by taste, advertising, fashion, politics, fear and greed. Why else would commercial advertising be the big business it is?

### Can Your Taste In Marriage Change?
### Absolutely!

This is as true in marriage as it is in car styles or fashion. We can be influenced by the culture to adopt certain thoughts, feelings and actions, even if they are not consistent with our basic character, morals or beliefs.

Despite this fact, there are *certain beliefs inside of you* that have been with you almost all of your life. They might very well be completely unconscious to you, but they are absolutely the biggest influences in how you think, feel and act in your life.

### For example, money: "The root of all evil?"

This is true about money. Your view of money, wealth, and your own personal value in relation to the amount of money you have will most certainly influence your thoughts, feelings and actions around acquiring and keeping wealth.

If—down deep inside of you—you have thoughts (and most of us do) such as "money is the root of all evil," "being rich spoils you and turns you into a mean and greedy person," and "the wealthy are all crooks," believe me this will influence your desire for and efforts toward acquisition of wealth.

### "But I Want To Be Rich!" You Say
### Do You? Or Does It Make You Terribly Nervous?

If you have this basic thought or belief driving you from the inside, when you do get money, you'll spend it as fast as you can, and get deep into debt and never get wealthy. You'll have a negative view of those who have great wealth and skepticism about their character. And most importantly, you'll never become wealthy because you'll be too busy judging the rich folks and avoiding becoming one yourself. You'll wonder "where it all went," and I can tell you: *It went into the pit of your beliefs and got swallowed up!*

Don't think for a minute you have conquered or are not influenced by the thought, "money is the root of all evil," if indeed you are not substantially wealthy (and even then, you might find yourself suddenly without it because of this belief system). What you believe about money (or anything else in this world) will be immediately apparent in your thoughts, feelings and behaviors.

Your lifestyle demonstrates your beliefs.

Whatever amount of wealth you currently have is a perfect reflection of your beliefs about wealth.

To become wealthy, you have to have an understanding of how you think, feel and believe about money and wealth. Change this basic view, if the one you have in place is in the way, and then change your behavior so that you can allow yourself to become wealthy, and be effective in the acquisition and keeping of wealth.

## The "Dirty Little Secrets"
## About "Dirty Little Secrets"

The same is true in terms of sex.

If you believe—even a little bit—that "sex is dirty," down deep, unconsciously, your sex life can never be ultimately satisfying in marriage or long-term relationships. Sooner or later, you'll notice that your sex drive goes away and you no longer find sex passionate and exciting in your marriage.

People think that the "new wears off" in sex. But what's really happening is that your model of sexuality is stuck, and that you've already experienced in the early stages of marriage going away from your basic model of sex (and your Marriage Blueprint regarding sex), and the rubber band is snapping you back to the view you really have about sex!

If you once believed that "sex is dirty" somewhere inside of you that belief is going to have power and influence your thoughts, feelings, and actions, whether you know it or not.

Sure, there are hormonal changes that take place which reduce sex drive, but the effect of these is way over-rated in terms of sexual interest, passion, and satisfaction.

Once a girl asked her mother, "when does a woman stop being interested in sex?"

The mother replied, "I don't know, ask your grandmother."

She asked her grandmother, who responded with a twinkle in her eye, "run along to your house and ask me later, your grandfather is coming home soon."

### So, Consider Whether Your Model of Marriage
### Supports Your Having a Great Marriage
### And Helps You EXPECT A Great Marriage

#### "If Things Aren't Working"

If things aren't working, then the problem is usually that your model of marriage and family ("blueprints") and that of your partner are in conflict!

When you truly understand the underlying dynamic driving your unhappiness, you won't have to be constantly struggling to get it right, you'll know what to do differently, how and why.

# CHAPTER SEVEN

## How to Handle Your Differences
## Using the Power of *The Intimacy Paradox*
### *(Do Mental Disorders Actually Exist?)*

I recognize that there are people who have true mental problems, such as schizophrenia or bipolar disorder-depression or ADD, etc. Sure.

But mental health diagnosis has gotten out of hand! It seems like every common sense challenge in the world now has a corresponding diagnosis.

After 25 years of doing psychotherapy and working with people from many walks of life from age 3 to 93, I feel prepared to tell you that I don't think there is very much validity in the model of mental illness.

*I do believe that there are large numbers of very unhappy people!*

But I fully believe that the source of their unhappiness is in most cases due to one thing—which is the disconnect between who you are inside and how you operate in the world.

### If You Are Suffering, Here's Why:
### You Aren't Handling Your Freedom Well

There is a conflict between what you think, feel and believe inside of you—and what you feel the world and others require or demand of you.

**The reason you suffer is because you haven't found a way to be the person on the outside that you are on the inside. Solve that and you solve your suffering and create endless happiness.**

It's that conflict between the inner world and the outer world that causes the majority of *personal* psychological pain and discomfort in the world.

People say they love freedom, but what they really like is the concept of freedom. Few people are prepared to really handle freedom. This is evident in the ways that people in "free" countries handle money (credit), food (obesity), sex and other choices they can make—statistically not very well.

**The big secret to living with freedom and happiness**
**In RELATIONSHIPS**
**is answering this challenge:**

*Be 100% who you really are*
*and accept others 100% for who they are.*

This is the secret to happiness, and if you don't get anything else from this book other than this truth, it's worth the price of admission thousands of times over. *It's the essence of everything I'm teaching.*

Perhaps it sounds obvious.

But the majority of people have no idea how to do it and even fewer truly accept it.

Most of us go around spending most of our time finding some reason not to accept others, finding ways to criticize their behavior or complain about how they are making us uncomfortable or upset.

**Want to be happy?** Do what the great and truly happy people do. Stop criticizing others and stop finding fault in them.

In this book, whose title I remind you is *You Don't Have To Change Who You Are To Have a Great Marriage,* the other, "unspoken" part of that is "you don't have to change who your spouse is" either!

You'd better not be trying to change him or her.

What you should be doing instead is working on 100% acceptance of who they are. This means accepting their personality, their beliefs, their views, their vulnerabilities and strengths, and knowing that all of that is their best answer to the challenges of life as of this moment.

You only have two other choices if you aren't willing to accept your spouse 100%.

The first line choice is to go to www.TenDaysToAGoodMarriage.com and get the book and work together on changing some behaviors.

The second choice is to face honestly you don't want to accept your spouse for who he or she is. In this case, you should go to www.CouplesCoach.com, to the section about divorce, and get really educated.

**Just don't go around being unhappy, hating yourself and others, or being critical or wallowing in self-pity. Taking action is far preferable, even if it seems frightening or daunting.**

Are you the victim of your own nagging critical voice? Do you criticize yourself and judge yourself? Most people do. It just isn't necessary. It's a total waste of time and vampires everything strong, good and productive out of you. Stop doing it.

**If you find things about your behavior or actions you don't like, it's more than likely because you aren't living up to your own values, beliefs and expectations for yourself.**

Answer: do something different.

### The Best Place to Start In Love of Self and Others

You'll find that as I am talking with you about differences between you and other people, you will naturally start looking at others with less critical eyes—finding more tolerance and acceptance of others and who they are—despite how different they may appear.

The closer you get to finding the magic code to both 100% acceptance of your partner and 100% acceptance of yourself, the better you will feel, and the less daunting and overwhelming life is going to seem to you. You will find that even though you and your spouse are different in some ways, you discover that you like and are curious about who they are.

**Don't tell me about what's wrong,** bad, unacceptable about them—how your husband doesn't listen to you, how your wife nags at you, how your husband doesn't seem interested or romantic anymore, how your wife withholds sex from you, and just talks endlessly to her friends, all of this kind of thing creates a picture in your mind of someone who is unacceptable and deserving of criticism.

There are reasons he doesn't listen, she nags, he isn't interested in romance anymore, and the rest of it. The reasons will become more and more apparent to you throughout the rest of this book, but the main reason is that you haven't accepted their Marriage Blueprint, and they haven't accepted yours.

You are living in lies if you believe that something is wrong with you or your spouse. Nothing is wrong with you or your spouse.

When you diagnose somebody as "sexually addicted," "a compulsive shopper," "a nag," "bipolar," "A.D.D.," "a hypochondriac," "a jerk," or use any other label, you have imprisoned them in a room from which there is no exit. You have excluded them from intimacy with you. You have denied them any possibility of being your intimate partner.

You formed a negative view of your spouse from which they can't be free and can never be a full partner to you. It's your job to change your mental picture of your partner, and to decide how you are going to respond to him or her. It is not your job to go around correcting what you see as a problem in your spouse.

Your spouse's answers to life's challenges are the best solutions they have come up with so far.

**Every person is sacred.**

**Every point of view is sacred.**

**Holy and Right.**

**Period.**

The human mind is a *solution-producing machine.* It's incredible how we can process the vast amount of data that comes flying at us all the time.

**Every solution the mind comes up with is a perfect solution— for the moment it is developed.**

Let me explain. If bombs are falling on my village, my mind will automatically scan my image of the village and seek the best place to be protected and then will set my feet running toward that spot. That's the best possible solution for the moment.

If my environs as a child are extremely loud and there's no privacy at all, my mind may be able to provide and discover a way of turning off the outside world in order to feel quiet inside, despite what is going on around me.

If I grow up in a family and place that is quite sedate with very little going on, and I have a dynamic and curious soul, my mind will find all kinds of interesting things to think about and investigate in that situation. The human mind has the ability to create its own separate world within the larger world.

**The Human Mind is a Solution Creating Machine.**
**It Never Shuts Down**
**The Human Mind is Infinitely Creative**
**Every Solution It Creates is Perfect**
**According to the Challenges You Put To It!**

*The human mind is just like that.* When we talk about the formation of beliefs and about the formation of your Marriage Blueprint, I'll show you just how your mind created that Blueprint, the exact process you used, and how this was the perfect solution for you at the time, and how it may or may not be the perfect solution for you now.

**You can literally form, create and live the marriage you want using this method!**

### Will You Be a Good Student
### In Order To Have a Great Marriage?

- You will clearly that you can get all the joy, love and satisfaction out of your marriage, by understanding the options available to you
- You will clearly see solutions instead of problems
- You will look for results and successes rather than for failures.

You might very well be looking for evidence of failure far more than you are seeking evidence of success right now. Most people are surprised when they actually look at the ratio of **success seeking** they are currently engaged in compared to the **failure or problem seeking** they are engaged in.

If you are complaining about or failing at anything in your Marriage (or in any other part of your life), you have an extremely active Failure Seeking Mechanism running inside of you—which you can simply re-focus.

### TUNE In to the Find Success Channel
### TUNE OUT of the Find Failure Channel
**Take Out Your Remote Control Right Now And Change Channels!**

- Your mind is tuned to the "Find Failure" Channel if you are finding failure.

- All you have to do is tune it to the "Find Success" Channel.

Energy is coursing through you all the time, and your only job is to learn how to direct it.

There's a joke that's pretty old by now, you might have heard it. What does it take to fly a Boeing 747 (the huge commercial airliners)? The answer: It takes a man and a dog. The man's job is to feed the dog and the dog's job is to bite the man's hands if he tries to touch anything.

The "man" in this story is your Failure Seeking Channel. I'm going to get you not only to make sure the dog bites the man's hand if he tries to mess with your Success Seeking Channel, but also to make sure the Success Seeking Mechanism is turned on and active all the time.

## Here's One of the Programs Now Playing
## On The Find Success Channel:

Cut out any man-bashing or woman-bashing you have been doing. Even focusing on differences—ones which scientists can identify with their microscopes or social scientists can identify by "counting the number of words uttered by men v. women in a day" will take you off the road to true intimacy. These "differences" are detours. They only serve to limit your brain and make it very hard for you to have intimacy.

If you focus on problems and differences, you will see problems and differences. If you focus on solutions and similarities, you will see solutions and similarities.

**TRUTH:** When it comes to relationships, the so-called differences between men and women are minimal—if they even exist at all.

Here's what I've found after 25 years of working with couples:

- Men have plenty of wisdom, skill, understanding and ability to be in a Great Marriage.
- Women have plenty of wisdom, skill, understanding and ability to be in a Great Marriage.

  Frankly, I see very little difference (if any) between men and women on this level—the level of our core beings.

- **Everyone, whether man or woman, wants the exact same things: love, understanding and respect.**

It doesn't have to be any more complicated than that.

Let's all stop man-bashing and woman-bashing. At our core we are all the same.

Sure, the ways SOME men and SOME women want love, understanding, and respect to be shown to them may differ. SOME men want these to be expressed primarily through sex and approval of their efforts. SOME women want these to be expressed primarily through being admired, given affection and feeling secure.

But just as many men want what we culturally assume women want, and just as many women want what we culturally assume men want.

It's nowhere near as cut and dried, as many comedians would have us think it is. "Men are_____," "Women are_____."

That's just nonsense in the real, live world.

What it comes down to is this, we ALL want the same things at heart, and that is to be truly loved, accepted and understood.

In all our glorious differences and similarities.

These glorious differences and similarities are represented in our Marriage Blueprints and how we handle them.

**I have not observed one single improvement in male-female relations as a result of any of the attempts to describe the differences between men and women, and I defy you to demonstrate any improvements you have seen!**

### There is No "Right Way" to be Married

There are 8 Marriage Blueprints including 4 "basic directions" and 2 *styles* each. These 8 Blueprints cut across all lines of culture and all ages as well as all periods of history, and only describe the basic patterns of marriage models. There are infinite variations in individual marriages!

When you really see the variety of models available, it will peel your eyes open about marriage for perhaps the first time.

And the amazing thing is that you can completely change the direction of your marriage through this information.

People are constantly evolving, changing and becoming new in their views, feelings, thoughts and beliefs. And although your Family Marriage Blueprint will stay the same, your Personal Marriage Blueprint is constantly changing, developing, and revising.

## No one has a monopoly even on what Marriage itself is!

If we are ever going to get past war, misunderstanding, hatred, fighting, conflict or disillusionment, we will have to get past the idea that anyone has the single, solitary truth on anything.

### Let's work hard to recognize
### That everyone has a piece of the truth,
### And no one has the WHOLE truth.

Let's recognize that some truth exists in every sincere and authentic point of view. Some people are, of course, insincere and only trying to mess with others. But even in this case, there can be some truth involved. Every statement ever made by a single person on earth throughout the entirety of human existence has had some nugget of truth in it.

So the path I'm asking you to join me on is one of discovery and understanding, leaving no one behind.

### Basic Requirement: Openness to Learning Something New

You know at the amusement parks where they have a bar at the entrance of the rides that says, "You must be this tall to go on this ride?"

Well, that's true here.

You must "be *this tall* in order to on this ride," and your "height" will be the amount of defensiveness and closed-mindedness you have. If your mind is closed and you are defensive about opening it up to others, you obviously cannot solve the Intimacy Paradox: 100% acceptance of self and 100% acceptance of others. You access to intimacy, and thus to a great marriage, is sealed in this case.

What we are going to discuss now is Defensiveness and being defensive, and how you must nip this completely in the bud before we go even one step further.

# CHAPTER EIGHT

## Kill Defenses before They Spread and Kill Your Marriage!

## (Requirement for Going on The Intimacy Ride!)

Get out your can of bug spray and kill it. Once it isn't moving anymore, stomp on it!

Don't maim it, kill it.

Hunt it down, and kick its derriere into the dark place it came from.

It's called "defensiveness." It's when you over-react to what your partner is saying or doing. You take things too personally, far too seriously, get hurt too easily and work far too hard to explain yourself and justify you reactions. You know you do, and you know it is a relationship killer!

But you think it's justified. "He's just so mean and unkind I have to protect myself." "She criticizes me so much I feel beaten down, and I have to come to my own rescue!"

You have to stop doing that.

If you are going to be married to your spouse, it's time for you to decide:

> - *Is your spouse's intention toward you good, and you are over-reacting, or*
> - *Are they **really out to get you?***

If you think your spouse is really out to get you, and is dangerous to you and/or your family, then do the logical thing: get out of the marriage. Divorce. Make a bold decision. Be rational.

But if you believe your spouse is sincere, and truly has your and your family's best interests in mind, then your choice is that you need to stop over-reacting to whatever he or she says. **Stop trying to reform THEIR behavior, and start reforming YOURS!**

If you are intend to stay, AND you want intimacy and a Great Marriage, then your only choice is to stop over-reacting to what your partner says and does.

You have to "kill" you defensiveness and over-reactions and get your mind, heart and soul clear. You have to stop all those over-reactions and pity parties that stop the relationship like a bucket of cold water.

Get ready to drop the defensiveness, or you are fired!

Ready to go on the **Ride of Intimacy?** Let's find out.

---

### You Must Be This Tall (Mentally) To Go On This Ride

#### *What's YOUR Mental Measurement?*
#### *Which one of these describes you?*

- *No Defensiveness (over-reaction) At All (Extremely Tall Mentally: Totally Open and Compassionate); having 100% acceptance of yourself and 100% acceptance of your partner. Almost NEVER over-reacting. You almost never take anything personally or feel hurt by anything said or done by your partner. You simply accept the differences between you and don't react when they show up.*

- *Very Limited Amount of Defensiveness (Very Tall Mentally: Quite Open). You almost never take anything personally or over-react to what your spouse says or does.*

- **A Little Defensive, a Little Skeptical, But Open (Mentally tall: Ready To Hear, a Little Cautious). You aren't taking most things personally, you aren't over-reacting, you are staying centered and calm. You have to be at least THIS TALL!**

- *Pretty Darned Defensive and a Bit Cynical (Very Short-Sighted and Closed to Others); You react strongly to almost everything that your spouse says with a feeling of being hurt or misunderstood. You defend yourself almost all the time.*

---

> • *Completely Defensive and Cynical (a Mental Midget);*
> *reacting at he slightest provocation or no provocation at all.*
> *Totally reactive.*

If you are **A Little Defensive, a Little Skeptical, But Open (Mentally Tall: Ready To Hear, a Little Cautious),** you might be ready to go on this ride! You have to be at least that "tall!" If you aren't, work on it!

Actually few people are even that open.

We fool ourselves all the time.

### Defensiveness is the Big Killer of All Intimate Relationships!

Why? It's because it stops all conversation and movement toward intimacy. When you over-react to your spouse or anyone else, you shut down the conversation, the feelings between you, and simply stop any intimacy.

→ **It isn't your spouse getting in the way of the intimacy with their actions. It's YOU getting in the way with your RE-ACTIONS!**

First, let's define "Defensiveness." Then let's go through 4 steps to understand it and how to reduce its impact on your Marriage, so you can reduce your reactions and reduce how much you take things personally!

- Why and how we develop Defenses and Reactions
- The Bad Effects of Defensiveness
- Why Intimate Relationships and Marriages Require Lowering of Defenses in Order to Thrive
- How to Lower Your Defenses and Enter Into Intimate Marriage

### Defensiveness: What is it? Here are some definitions:

When we feel that something or someone is threatening in our world—such as criticism or negativity coming at us in our relationships, **we try to blunt the impact of that by doing four things. We might:**

- Block its access to us by hardening ourselves, closing down our senses and mind and **not being accessible** to the thing that threatens us—literally going deaf.

---

- **Change the topic** or subject to something we feel comfortable about, called re-directing the energy. If it's about sex and we feel uncomfortable, we change the topic to whatever we like such as to television shows or music.
- **Leave the room or the relationship. Pure avoidance.**
- **Try to force instructions** from our spouse on what we should "do about it," in order to have something to do and thus be able to distract the onslaught of energy coming at us. We might get "orders" from the other person so that *we can then totally disregard* them because they are nuts.

## Defensiveness is learned in 3 stages
## And Then, Unfortunately, Can Become a Life Habit, Like an Addiction

1. At some time, you are literally criticized, yelled at, punished, hit or slapped physically or verbally. You don't like it! And you want to get away from it! You fear it happening again!
2. You don't like feeling bad or that you "are bad." You have to do something to stop feeling bad! So you choose to fight back, hide and avoid the pain or try to explain yourself. You just don't want that bad feeling again! You are doing everything you can to "ward it off."
3. When you grow up and you feel a "perceived attack" coming your way, you immediately begin throwing the energy back at the other person. You complain or criticize right back; you refuse to accept the criticism. You shut the other person out and regard them with scorn or even contempt. You refuse to accept the criticism. Or you simply shut down!

**However, when you are defensive, you do four really bad things to your spouse:**

1. You Stop Listening.
2. You Dismiss What They Say As Irrelevant.
3. You Hide Inside Of Yourself or Avoid Contact.
4. You Protect Yourself Unnecessarily.

Unless your spouse is really dangerous and you are in imminent, literal physical danger, you have to stop doing these things in order to have a Great Marriage. If they are a real danger, GET OUT OF THERE!

### I Understand, You Don't Want To Feel Bad!

In all cases, defensiveness starts out as something that our resourceful mind has invented to protect us and make us feel good and not bad. We hate to feel bad, so we have come up with this marvelous repertoire of things that we call defensiveness in order not to feel bad. Very creative solution to a threatening problem.

The big problem is that we continue to use defensiveness not only when something bad is coming at us (to keep from feeling bad); but also we eventually train ourselves to head off the potential criticism, hurt or punishment from coming our way (in order not to feel bad), BEFORE IT EVEN STARTS HAPPENING!

This is a problem.

When your spouse hasn't even STARTED criticizing or complaining to you about you, you are already putting up a defense.

This means that no real communication can take place at all.

It's just plain blocked.

When communication is blocked to that level, it's usually certain that very little joyous connection is going to be taking place. To feel joy, connection and intimacy, you have to deliberately and consciously lower your defenses.

### How to Lower Your Defenses

It's very possible to lower your defenses if you know the three steps outlined here.

**First Step:** Notice that you are being defensive and blocking intimacy.

**Second Step:** Decide (**DECIDE**) to think the following: "My partner is questioning and criticizing me in order to have a Great Marriage. It might not be what I think should be happening, but it's what he or she thinks will help. I'm going to decide to receive the criticism, complaint or questioning from this viewpoint. I will not over-react or feel hurt, but instead remain open to what is being said to me!

Example: Your spouse says to you, "You never are on time."

You don't defend against it. You don't explain yourself, you don't lash out, you don't get mad and you don't pout. You learn from it and open yourself up to your partner's view of you. You accept the statement as something that your spouse has felt important to bring up.

You simply ask, "How is it for you to have a spouse who is never on time?"

What's so hard about that? Nothing! That is, if you aren't feeling defensive, personally attacked or hurt. When you can stop feeling personally attacked by your spouse, you are ready for greater intimacy.

## Lesson from Gurdjieff's Father

The famous spiritual rascal Gurdjieff tells the story of what his father helped him learn. When someone insulted his father, Gurdjieff says, his father said, "Sir, I will consider your criticism for 24 hours. If I find truth in it, I will be back to speak with you. If I do not, I will not be back to speak with you."

If he found truth in the statement, he returned to the person who had criticized him and said, "thank you for pointing out the error of my ways! I do appreciate your taking the time and consideration of pointing it out to me."

If he found no truth in the statement, he simply acknowledged that there might be something he didn't understand about what the person said, but that his own understanding was too limited to grasp the criticism. In which case, he made no response but continued to smile at the person and kindly acknowledge him when he saw him again around the village.

When you start doing this, you'll START being ready for a Great Marriage. Be prepared to accept your spouse's comments (or even criticisms) about you with genuine openness and receptivity. If there is something of value in what you hear, discover and express gratitude for it! This has a magical effect on the way you see the "data" coming at you from outside.

**Third Step:** Consistently apply the principle of lowering your defenses.

- Don't defend yourself (you don't need to).
- Don't explain your actions (You don't need to).

- Accept your spouse's criticisms of you as valid attempts on her or his part to have a better marriage with you (very good).
- Ask about the impact of your actions on him or her, and find out exactly how you have hurt, offended or dismissed your spouse directly from his or her mouth (absolutely excellent).

**Lowering your defenses is a wonderful way of making yourself available for intimacy. The process has to start somewhere, so why not with you?**

You get lots of rewards when you do so. You get to feel better about yourself (because you are not going around explaining yourself, protecting yourself, fighting for your right to exist), and feeling less attacked or hurt. That's great, in itself.

Will your spouse start being kinder and more loving as a result of your being less defensive and taking things less personally? Maybe, and maybe not. Who knows? He or she may be so used to you over-reacting to everything that they simply don't believe you are doing something different. And just because you become less defensive doesn't mean that they will!

However, it does often happen that when ONE person starts doing something new (such as smoking cessation, dieting, having a spiritual practice, being kind), and genuinely and consistently continues to do this, **very frequently the other spouse starts changing his or her behavior.** A rising tide floats all boats! Work on raising your level and maybe your spouse will too!

Is it fair that you take the initiative? Sure! This way you can feel great about making this move. Stop personalizing what your spouse says to you, stop explaining yourself, and you'll feel better, less imprisoned by what you perceive as attacks, misunderstandings or unkindness.

You'll understand more about how to control and manage your defenses in Part II, which is about your belief systems, how you got them and how they run your life. As a matter of fact by the time you finish Part II, you may not feel defensive about anything, but rather, find that your mind is open in ways you've never experienced before!

# PART TWO

**What Makes You (And Your Spouse) Tick?**
Your Belief Systems—How You Got Them
How They Run Your Life,
And How You Can Create New "Belief Engines"

# CHAPTER NINE

## What Really Makes You—And Your Spouse—Tick

Now we are really going to dive into **exactly what makes you tick.** When you have finished this chapter you'll know a lot more about yourself, and exactly why and how you get the results you do in life, positive or negative!

There might be some areas of life you are *great in,* some you are good in, some you are mediocre in and some that you, well, "fall on your derriere" when you attempt.

For example, *you might be very good at making money,* but terrible at sustaining intimate relationships. You might be a very good and successful parent, but you can't seem to make any progress at work and are constantly on probation there.

You might be a good natural athlete, but you clutch when it comes to playing in a game. Or you might have an excellent memory for people, their names and pretty much everything they've ever told you, but you can't seem to remember to pay your bills.

Is success and satisfaction a matter of natural ability? It is about simply finding what you are already good at and developing it fully?

More to the point in our discussion in Marriage, is happiness in marriage just about finding someone "compatible" to you and then you'll live happily ever after—the "E-Harmony" model?

Doesn't natural ability come into play? Of course it does. In athletics, science, wealth building, research, teaching, parenting, being a mechanic, art, friendship; no matter what area of life you think about, it certainly seems that some people have a natural talent for being successful at what they do.

And many of us envy those "naturally talented" people, as if life is just much easier for them.

In marriage itself, *it just seems like some people "get lucky"* and meet the "love of their life" or "soul-mate," and then they seem to find it easy to get along and have a great marriage afterwards.

## "Natural Talent Is Really Over-Rated"

"Natural talent" is a gift, we might think of it as a gift from God, or your "God-given talents." However, this concept is greatly overrated; or better said; natural ability itself is greatly overrated as a measure of success.

Many highly successful people in all walks of life actually have very mediocre or average talents in the area of their success. But they had some magic key—which they often did not understand themselves—which drove them to do the things that made them successful.

## It's Not Because You Have the "Wrong Methods"
## Methods Are Easy
## It's about Tuning In To The Right Channel

If you are not achieving what you want to achieve in your life, it's not about your having the wrong methods.

- If you are trying to lose weight, another diet will not help you unless you have the key. If you haven't lost weight on the last 4 diets you attempted, you won't lose weight on the next diet you try.
- If you have been trying to be more successful in business and managing your time and have been consistently unsuccessful, it wouldn't matter if Stephen Covey himself came over to your office and spent the next two months with you as his single focus. *It wouldn't matter unless you have the key.*
  The minute Stephen Covey left your office you'd be right back where you were before, *if you don't have the key.*
- If you've been trying to learn a new skill, such as a foreign language, and have been unsuccessful up to this time, no matter

what program you try, or how long you live in a foreign country to try to learn the language, *you won't ever be very successful unless you have the key.*

- And if you are in a marriage and you'd like it to be a Great Marriage, and no matter how hard you or your partner try, no matter how many books or manuals or workshops you go to; no matter how much therapy you get; no matter how much your pastor or rabbi exhorts you on what you should do; no matter how many Dr. Phil shows you watch, you still seem to do nothing but struggle when you try to talk to one another, the problem is that you don't have the key.

### What is this key?

**The key is having the kind of belief that drives your actions to success.** I'm not talking necessarily about religious belief! I'm talking with you about your beliefs and conclusions about YOU in reference to what you are trying to do, achieve, be, think or feel.

There are things you do well and things that currently you don't do so well, right? And wouldn't you like to be able to do anything you undertake and really want to achieve, and get the best and most satisfying results possible?

Interestingly, if you get this key in *one area of Life*, you'll see how it can be used to open up **all areas of your Life.**

Why is it true that there's such a difference in your level of success in different areas of your life? Why are you so successful in one area of life and not in others? Let's find out.

### Why You Do What You Do

Please answer these questions.

What drives you to do what you do in your life? What's most important to you in your life? What is your motivation to achieve, and what makes you happy and alive and satisfied?

- Would you say it's money and building wealth?
- Would you say it's having a family and protecting and nurturing your children?

- Would you say it's helping other people?
- Would you say it's solving intellectual puzzles?
- Is it creating beautiful and meaningful art?
- Is it being able to fix things, such as machines, that no one else can fix?
- Is it bringing the truth of your religion to other people?
- Or is it something else that you think drives you to achieve what you do? What are the most important values you serve?

Now, let me ask you how well you do at these things? Are you successful at them?

Would you like to be more successful at everything you want to achieve?

If so, you'll have to go a little deeper.

You'll have to really understand two things that are behind and really are the source of your interests, and how well you succeed in those things.

- The first is what I call Your Family Belief System (what you absorbed as a kid).
- The second is what I call Your Personal Belief System (what you developed on your own).

In marriage, for example, you'll see that you have a set of Family and Personal Beliefs about marriage: what it is to you, what you expect and think is possible, what you think marriage is and what you think it should be for you.

How about seeing the power of beliefs in action with my client James?

# CHAPTER TEN

## How James Got Deeply Depressed
## And Then Instantly "Un-depressed"

Everyone who is alive was born in a particular location and had people and things around them as a baby and small child and through adolescence. A lot is going on around you as you grow up!

Your mother and father were there and maybe nearby some siblings and other relatives, friends of the family, neighbors.

There is television, radio, stereos, movies, books. There are acquaintances, strangers, classmates, teachers, pastors. There are grocery stores, department stores, billboards, people interacting.

There's a lot of stuff going on around you all the time.

I read last year that the **average American experiences 1,531 individual commercial solicitations** a day, hears 25,000 or more words a day. The average American watches over 3.5 hours of television a day, in addition to listening to music either on the radio (more ads), MP3 player, satellite radio, and goodness knows how many other sounds of human activity that we hear either on the obvious or subtle level as we go about our days.

**That's a lot of influence,** that's a lot of data coming at us, from the moment we are born and throughout our lives.

And it's not surprising that most people feel very tired at night, and yet don't sleep very well.

Take all that and add the influence of caffeine, alcohol, prescription drugs, heavy sugar and salt intake, fast foods with high fat content and continuous demands of work, bills and other responsibilities that most people carry each day, and you end up with a person who is at the receiving end of a lot of stimulation.

**Day in, day out, influencing factors are coming from your environment toward you.** If you feel overwhelmed by all of this and kind of driven into a trance, that's what most people feel also, so you're not alone.

However, let's think of all this another way.

- Let's call _all_ this information (words, images, television programs, music, conversations, neighborhood sounds, etc.) that's coming at you "data."

That's all it really is.
_It's just "data."_

- **Anything that you do with this data coming at you, let's call your "response."**

So there is a constant movement of data toward you throughout your life, and then your response to it.

Why is this important? Because what you DO with this determines how your life goes. Because your emotional and physical reactions to the data coming in at you determine every result you get in your life. It determines who you are and what you become. It determines exactly how you feel about your life, what you think about your life and the results you get in your life!

**Your reaction**—thoughts, feelings, body sensations, imagination, and actions—to the data coming at you **is, surprisingly, mostly under your control.**

How can that be true?

Because every piece of information you get is processed through your own internal filters and sent into a category in your brain which we call your beliefs.

If you like a "flowchart" version of this, here it is:

---

_**DATA → goes into your senses →**_
_**Gets processed by your thinking, categorized by beliefs →**_
_**Generates feelings (happy, sad, angry, afraid, etc.) →**_
_**Drives your actions and what you do with the data →**_
_**Which further confirms your Beliefs**_

---

## James And His Depression Generating Belief System

James came to his first therapy session with me. He told me he was quite depressed and wanted to get over this depression. He was, he said, "sick and tired of being sick and tired."

He had already had a thorough medical exam and he had been found to be in excellent physical condition. His cardiovascular system was excellent, since he was a very athletic person. His cholesterol levels were enviable. He slept well and had a good relationship with his wife and grown children and grandchildren. He had all the money he needed and rewarding work that he was proud of.

He had been on a strong dose of one of the new antidepressants and told me that the only thing it did was make him feel a little spacey, and ended up taking a couple of hundred dollars a month out of his pocket.

Yet he felt very depressed. He said that every day he felt worse, more hopeless and more tired. He feared that if he went on this path much longer he would start to feel very hopeless and he feared that he wouldn't want to live anymore.

I asked him to tell me about the day that he had so far, what he did, said, saw and thought.

He told me that he had gotten up early and worked out before breakfast. I asked him about thoughts, feelings and how his body felt doing that. He said that even though he was working out, he was acutely aware of the fact that he was now 53 years old and he was computing how many years he had to live at best. It made him wonder what was the use of keeping in great condition, if he was just going to die in so many years from now anyway.

### What's the Use? Only Six Years to Live

When I asked him about the age at which his father died, he said, 59 years old. I asked him if this meant he had only about 6 years to live and he said that this was utter nonsense. But it was clear that he was preparing to die in about 6 years. His belief system is that men in his family don't make it to 60. I don't care what he says, this is what he believes. Not only that, but they work their butts off (like his father did up to 59), and have nothing really to show for it (his father never achieved some of his important life goals).

Then he went inside and took a shower. On looking at himself in the mirror, he saw a man who had lost a lot of muscle definition (he hadn't really), and who was looking old already (he wasn't), and that probably pretty soon wouldn't even be able to do the thing he loved most, which was backpacking (extremely unlikely).

He ate breakfast and wondered whether the food he was consuming was the right kind of food for him, and whether he wasn't in fact eating just the wrong things that might lead to him feeling very ill.

He watched a few minutes of the news on television and thought *"the world is going to hell.* All the politicians do is lie to us and I can't see how our country can last more than 20 more years if we go on with the same economic policies we have." He chose to watch the news channel which is the very best at splashing lurid and sensationalist headlines across the screen. Then he saw a commercial for a large SUV and thought about how much damage humans have done to the earth's environment.

Then he went to the post office. I asked him what he saw when he went there. He said that while waiting in line to pick up a package, all he saw was old people and fat people who looked like they had bad hygiene, and that were probably picking up their disability checks and leeching off the government and decent taxpayers like him.

Of course, when he got to his office, all he saw was people avoiding work and trying to escape responsibilities and being completely ineffective and getting away with everything they could. No need to go into details here, you get the picture, right?

And, you guessed it, when he got home, he was greeted by his wife, who seemed to be able to think of nothing but things James had forgotten to do or should have fixed by now, or what kind of bills they needed to pay that were becoming overdue. All James could think about in looking at her was how old she was looking and wondering if he would run out of sexual interest in her soon.

### So what's causing his depression?

I think it will be obvious to you when I'm talking about James but perhaps not so obvious if I were talking with you about what might be making you feel bad.

Is it that the world is just a depressing place? Some people might say so, or secretly think so. Or is the world a wonderful, vibrant, joyous place and he's just not seeing it?

### The Key to Beliefs and Their Power

### But here's that famous KEY I was talking about.
### It Has 4 Parts.

1. The world, people, you and I, events that take place—all the data that comes at us is neutral. It only has meaning when we assign it meaning according to our Beliefs.

2. Our Beliefs determine everything about our responses—thoughts, feelings and bodily experiences—to the neutral data that comes our way.

3. We only see the data that confirms our expectations.

4. How we interpret the data that comes at us determines our success, failure, happiness and unhappiness, satisfaction and joy in life.

Now I want to make something clear before we go one more step. I'm not advocating mere "positive thinking."

I'm not about to tell you to think positive thoughts only about the world and yourself and you'll be a success and happy. That's nonsense.

Thinking positively is not necessary.

There is no single way to be successful and happy.

What you CAN do, however, is to find out if something works for you, whether it serves your purposes and put your attention, focus and personal energy into that thing rather than into other things.

What matters are only 2 things:

1. Does your belief system **get the results** you want to get?

2. Do you feel happy and "in the Zone" with your belief system?

I can tell you that our friend James was NOT getting the results he wanted, and that he was not happy and not in the Zone with his belief system.

## James Was Tuned Into *The Failure Channel!*

He had a set of negative and self-defeating beliefs that were working overtime inside of him.

This set of Beliefs included:

- I'm at the age where death comes soon to men in my family.
- Because I'll die soon, nothing has much meaning.
- Other people are lazy and looking for the way out.
- There's really not much more in the world than bad news.
- All I do in life is struggle against the odds and try to be happy
- People are always demanding things of me and are never satisfied.
- I'll never be happy or joyous, and what's the use anyway if I'm going to die soon.

Here's the wacky thing.

Even when I pointed out all these beliefs operating behind the scenes in his life, he denied that he had any of them. He said, "I don't really believe I'm going to die at 59"—but his thoughts, feelings and actions demonstrated clearly that indeed he DOES believe (or part of him believes totally) that he's going to die at 59, and that thought runs his life in the background.

**It doesn't matter whether he accepts this consciously or not.**

He had put a "thinking" filter that I call a Personal Belief System over the top of his Family Belief System, which had worked for him for a long time, and helped him feel good about his world.

Unfortunately, he had been overwhelmed by a much older and more powerful belief system—his "Family Belief System"—and was completely under its spell and power.

I'll tell you exactly how James got "undepressed," and began to feel joy and pleasure in his life, a little later.

But first I have to tell you how **he got this set of Beliefs, and how you got your set of Beliefs.** I'll show you how you developed your Family Belief System and how you developed your Personal Belief System. And why this is so important to your life, and how you think, feel and experience it.

Take a deep breath. You're getting it! Even if this is brand new information to you or it seems a little overwhelming, it's all going to get easier as we go along. Your brain is creating a brand new map inside and having the experience of "seeing itself."

**You are looking right straight into the inner workings of your own brain.** Your brain has to process it, so it's kind of like your brain looking at itself. But wonderfully enough, the brain really enjoys this kind of attention and stimulation.

Already some profound changes are taking place inside of you which are going to make everything in your life work better, and help you get the results you want in everything you do!

And all you have to do is just keep following along. The powerful stuff is happening in the background, like a computer program doing all kinds of calculations that you don't see, but produce the cool images, websites or audio/video you see on your computer!

Read the following sentences very carefully because it is the key to your decision for happiness or unhappiness in life:

**Your Beliefs Are Manifested In The Thoughts, Feelings, Vision and Actions You Actually Perform in Life.**
**The Life You Have Is a True Picture of Your Beliefs.**

Your belief system is not something cut off from what you actually do in life. Your belief system IS what you actually do in life.

There are always two levels of beliefs operating in your life.

- The Deep, Unconscious "Family Belief System"
- And the Conscious "Personal Belief System."

### Your Family Belief System

Remember that we have all this data coming at us all the time that I said is neutral until we do something with it, interpret it and translate it? We decide whether something is good or bad according to whether it fits our categories of "good" or "bad."

Reminder: **Data coming in is Neutral. Our interpretation of that data makes it positive or negative.**

Many people who at one time were called "rebels" and "outlaws" were later considered pioneers, liberators and freedom fighters.

Many people who were at one time called "martyrs for the cause" were later considered crooks and phonies.

**It depends on your filter.**

Everything that you experience (information inside your brain or stimuli coming at you) is neutral until you assign it meaning.

What is happening all the time is that among all the data that is coming our way, we are constantly sorting through that information for meaning.

It would be interesting to look at your life *in all areas,* and how you could have a different life, but for this book about having a Great Marriage, let's see how this process works in creating your Marriage Blueprint.

## Your Family Marriage Blueprint:
## An Example of a Family Belief System

The Marriage Blueprint is a set of thoughts, feelings and beliefs already established in your mind about what marriage is or should be.

## Where did you get your Family Marriage Blueprint?
## Well, Mostly from Your Family!

You got it from two places:

1. *From the outside.* From models you saw in your experiences with your parents and other adults who were married. From models you saw on television, in movies, through books, or through things you heard from people around you.
2. And more importantly, *from the inside.* From conclusions **that you made, based on the models you saw in your life.**

This last part is incredibly important.

*Everyone has experiences in life, but frequently two people will interpret those experiences quite differently*

---

*Even in a single family with kids, say, 18 months apart in age, two siblings might describe an extremely different picture of their family experience and their parents' marriage.*

*One kid might say:*
*"I'd never want to be like my parents, or have their kind of marriage. They fight all the time. They never get along. They*

---

*always seem to disagree about how the money should be spent, where we ought to go on vacation, whether we should move to a new place, whether we kids are given too much discipline or not enough, all kinds of things. My father is completely hen-pecked and my mother runs the show. I don't think that's the way it should be in a marriage. My mother always gets her way and my father never gets his. They are loud and noisy and embarrassing and I hate going anywhere with them."*

**And the other kid:**

*The other sibling, though perhaps only a year and a half older or younger might say about the exact same marriage, "I think my parents are very alive and interesting, and I'd love to have a marriage like theirs. They are always talking things through, even though it's a little confusing to hear how differently they think about how to spend money or vacations or how we kids ought to be disciplined. It makes me think a lot about how I'm going to be as a parent. They are funny and smart and seem to always disagree about everything, but in a way that keeps everything lively around our house. My father is very understanding and has never played 'macho man,' or tried to run my mother down. He always discusses every decision with my mother. My mother is very strong and outspoken, and ahead of her time in being a truly independent thinker. I admire the way my parents are able to both be individuals and still be a married couple."*

Do you see what happened?

Both people had the same "data" or information coming in. They agreed on the data.

- They agreed that their parents were making a lot of noise.
- They agreed that their father gave in to their mother.
- They agreed that their mother made her points and got her way a lot.

They had the **same parents,** and they were close enough in age that it wasn't terribly important or decisive in how they saw the parents.

They were kids, so they don't have advanced training in psychology, tons of life experience, or their own marriages to bank history upon.

They are taking the information that comes their way (parents making a lot of noise, etc.) and drawing some of their own conclusions about that information.

The first kid **concludes from observation that the parents are unhappy,** and in way too much conflict to have what he (she) would consider a Great Marriage. From this conclusion you can see that a whole cascade of thoughts, feelings and actions will likely take place.

### Kid #1 and His Conclusions:
### The Negative Belief System Generated
### Is This Like You?

I'll just use "he" in this example to make the sentences simple, but it could just as easy be "she."

- He has already concluded that good marriage should include harmony and getting along.

- He has concluded that people who are happy in marriage ought to see eye to eye on things, and not be fighting a lot. It should be "quiet around the house."

- He has concluded that there's likely to be some problem in gender roles, based on his observations between men and women. And that, at least in this case, **his father is doing too much compromising and that his mother is being too controlling.**

- He will probably view marriage as a place where conflict is a problem, and that marriage holds the threat of conflict and negative outcomes.

- **He will probably judge later relationships on the basis of whether they have a feeling of harmony he has already judged should be there in good marriages, or whether it is full of conflict, which he'll consider bad.**

And lots of other thoughts, feelings and decisions about actions in the future will come out of this seemingly simple observation.

These thoughts and feelings begin to congeal into a Marriage Blueprint, or a design about what marriage ought to be, and what he can expect, and how he should proceed in making decisions about marriage.

How and why did he come to these conclusions? Who knows and who cares? He just did.

**Is it the parents' fault or responsibility that he came to these conclusions and began to create this particular Marriage Blueprint? NO.**

People make up their own minds about marriage on the basis of all kinds of things, some of which are going on inside them (their physical response to situations, their mental processing, their age and place in the birth order, all kinds of things), and some of which are going on outside them (what their parents or others say and express about marriage, movies and television, books, advertisements, their friends and what they say, etc.).

This is, in part, what I mean by your Marriage Blueprint, though you'll see in much greater detail the 8 Marriage Blueprints, and all will come clear to you.

### What Kid # 2 Concluded
### FROM THE SAME DATA!

**The second kid concludes from observation that the parents are lively and energetic and that their "noise" is a sign of their being quite alive and exciting.** She would look forward to a marriage like this one, and, in fact, considers it to be a Great Marriage. From this conclusion you can see that a whole cascade of thoughts, feelings and actions will likely take place.

I'll use "she" in this example to make the sentences simple, but it could just as easily be "he."

- *She has already concluded that good marriage should include dynamic interaction and "noise" to be lively and interesting.*

- She has concluded that *people who are happy in marriage will speak their minds* and have their own opinions which they will feel free to express.

- She has concluded *that men and women can indeed have a marriage based on equality and respect,* and that her father is a good and positive model of what men can be in marriage, and that her mother is a good example of what women can be in marriage.

- She will probably view marriage as a place where *conflict or disagreement is seen as a good thing,* which keeps marriages alive and interesting.

- She will probably judge later relationships on the basis of whether they have this *feeling of liveliness* and equality she has already judged that there should be in marriages. Free exchange of differences will probably be considered the gold standard of communication, and if she's with a husband who doesn't challenge her and accept her challenges of him, she'll probably consider that to be unfulfilling in a marriage.

See? Same data, two very different conclusions.

Is one right and the other one wrong? Well, your answer depends on your Marriage Blueprint, doesn't it? And on your view of YOU in a marriage, as well as what the communication should look like.

I think you might be seeing at this point, that it's very possible that these two siblings have developed some pretty strong conclusions as kids about what marriage is or should be—and this is going to strongly influence the way they think, feel and act to some extent in their future plans for marriage!

### This is part of what I call the Family Marriage Blueprint

It's comprised of *two* parts.

1. Data or information coming in from "outside" of our skin— from parents, other adults, television, radio, books, advertising, music and many other sources, and

2. **What each of us DOES with this information,** and what value or meaning we assign to it.

"Loud parents who argue" means, in this situation, two completely different things to these two siblings, right?

Is this conclusion created by the parents and their actions? NO.

The conclusion and its contribution to the Marriage Blueprint being developed inside of each kid, results from an independent process that goes on regardless of the outside influences or data coming in.

**You make up your own mind about marriage and every other thing in life.**

And I've shown it a little differently than it actually happens.

It's usually much more sneaky and unconscious than this.

We have experiences of our parents' or other marriages, and make our conclusions about what marriage is, what we can expect and what it should be, mostly very unconsciously, and with very little thought.

**Most of us don't even think about it very much. The Blueprint is being drawn, and we only faintly see it or understand the power it has on us.**

That is until we find ourselves inexplicably right in the middle of our parents' marriage, which we perhaps never expected to happen. Remember how Neal and Rita (in the first chapter) were shocked to find out they were living out the exact blueprint of their parents' marriages?

The first kid in the example, who felt that harmony and seeing eye to eye in marriage is defined as good, suddenly finds himself with a woman who is always disagreeing with and provoking him, and is loud and opinionated. And he feels maybe he's landed in a bad marriage, and that it's a nightmare and he wonders how the devil that happened.

The second kid in the example, who felt that independence and having and expressing her own opinion—and having equality in relationship—suddenly finds herself with a man who expects her to give in to his opinions and agree with him, and calls her a "ball buster" because she disagrees, and she feels maybe she's landed in a bad marriage, and that it's a nightmare, and she wonders how the devil that happened.

Ever had the feeling that you are kind of destined to re-create exactly what you most dislike, as if you are caught in an Irony Machine which keeps churning out exactly what you don't like?

You're not alone in that feeling. Lots of people have it.

**Another important principle I want you to understand:**
**Beliefs, once established, never die!**
**You CAN'T KILL 'EM!**

Once a belief is established inside you (such as a Family Marriage Blueprint), it will continue to exist for the rest of your life. It will influence you for the rest of your life.

Example: If you grew up in a tough neighborhood and had to fight to live, you might have made an early conclusion that people shouldn't be trusted much, and that you have to fight to make it in this world. Some part of you, let's call it a Family Belief System, is going to believe this the rest of your Life.

Will you ever be able to plug in a new belief (such as that some people can be trusted and that it's OK to relax and not be fighting all the time), and live by it?

Sure, and we'll be talking about that and how to do it soon.

But what you need to understand is that your new or Personal Belief System will never be able to grab 100% of the available thinking, feeling and acting for itself.

**Your Family Belief System will always have some percentage of the available energy stored in it.** To some extent you will always be driven by and determined by it. End of story.

Let's say you are just walking along minding your own business, calm as can be, taking it easy. Some guy comes up and tries to assault you and take your money. Do you think you'll instantly be back into your Fighting Self (Your Family Belief System developed early in life)? You bet you will.

Will that be a good thing? It very well might be!

Would you like to continue living with all your energy into that Family Belief System—the Fighting Self?

I doubt it. Chances are you've discovered a brand new way to live that you like better, if you've developed a new Personal Belief System, which allows you to live a calmer and less aggressive life. Or maybe suddenly charging up the old Fighting Self feels great and you suddenly feel the desire to enter back into that life.

Can I tell you which is a better life for you? No way!

You have to decide that for yourself, and really consider what serves you best, and how you want to live.

### It's a matter of individual choice

The Family Belief System (like the Family Marriage Blueprint, for example) sets up a set of conditions in a belief system that is developed pretty early in life. It has a lot of power because of its longevity and persistence. All belief systems have something in common in that they try to find a way to express themselves.

Sometimes people talk about having ambivalence or "internal conflict" about decisions they make or conflicting points of view.

### Jerry and His Internal Fight over Money!
### Is Money Evil?
### If It Is, So What?

A man I know, Jerry, is a very accomplished day trader of futures in the U.S. Futures Markets. He makes a lot of money in his work. Interestingly, he was raised in a very orthodox Mennonite home where he was taught the value of living on a farm in a life of doing for yourself; he was taught very directly that money is evil and will ruin your life.

Jerry was directly taught that money is evil. Yet here he is living in the world of money!

He feels this conflict every day, and even though he is an accomplished capitalist and now is living in a luxury city apartment, he dreams of living in on a farm and raising animals, and has a feeling that he really *should be* living that life, instead of the one he is living.

**He's resolved the internal conflict** by establishing that in a certain number of years, he plans to move back to the country. He has already bought some land he plans to build on in a few years. And he is giving a large amount of money in trust to found a Mennonite mission.

He's very wisely recognized that his Family Belief System around money and how to live, is still very strong inside of him, and he hasn't tried to shut it down or ignore it. He's worked very hard to balance the "sides."

## His Old Belief System Never Died
## It Just Went Underground
## Now He Has Found a Way to Combine
## The Old Belief System with the New Belief System.
## This is How It's Done.

### It's Not About "Killing" An Old Belief System.

He's done a nice job of combining this Family Belief System with a new Personal Belief System that he developed and chose, which was to see money as a neutral thing in itself.

Somewhere, he once heard that having more money only makes you more of what you already are. So, for example, if you are a generous, thoughtful, and nice person to begin with, you'll have more opportunities to be generous, thoughtful and nice on a larger scale, if you simply have more money.

Sounded right to him, so he personalized this idea as part of a Belief System. The reason this works for him is that he's done a good job of balancing an old belief and a new belief, ignoring neither. As a matter of fact, he's applied his new Personal Belief to his Family Belief and worked out a wonderful understanding between these two seemingly paradoxical and conflicting beliefs.

You, too, can find a workable and effective balance between your Family Belief System and your Personal Belief System.

You can do that, if you expect to enjoy your time on earth.

Otherwise, you are going to be in a lot of "fights" inside of yourself, and always wondering why things "don't go your way."

# CHAPTER ELEVEN

## How Your Belief System Got
## Inside Your Brain and Can *Never Die*

### (James's Solution to His Depression)

Did you ever buy a new car and suddenly wonder why everyone else went out and bought one just like it?

They didn't, of course. You just started noticing because you had that model of car.

Pregnant couples suddenly notice that lots of people are having babies.

If you get a motorcycle, it's amazing how many motorcyclists you start seeing. Must be a fad, eh?

It's something that happens when your attention gets directed, you start seeing what you expect to see.

### You are scanning for "proof and evidence"
### To prove "your case."

Every belief system that you have developed does another very important activity inside your mind, soul and body. **It constantly scans the environment for evidence of its truth!**

Let's say that somewhere deep inside you *really believe* that people are untrustworthy, and that they will do anything to promote their own personal survival and profit, including taking advantage even of their best friends.

If you believe that deep inside of you—even if you are not aware of it at all, or even believe you've "gotten rid of it"—this Family Belief System (which has a life of its own) will continue to seek evidence of its truth.

### *BOING! Here it is again*

The first time someone cheats you, even just a little bit, on a money deal (even if it is a waiter giving you wrong change in a restaurant), you'll instantly feel the presence of this Family Belief, that people are not trustworthy and are out to use you!

It doesn't matter one bit if you think you've "gotten beyond it," and have become a yogic guru who preaches inner peace and acceptance to thousands of people who follow you with blind obeisance and hang on every word you say.

It doesn't matter if you are the Senior Pastor at Kingdom Come Church with a congregation of 25,000, you preach every day about loving and forgiving your neighbor, and believe you are washed by the Blood of the Lamb.

If you have this Family Belief, it's going to show up as a hard-wired belief, and can be very shocking in its power to control your thinking and feeling! This is why people are said to "suddenly snap" and commit murders, embezzle funds, or run off with redheads, when they "seemed like such nice steady guys" to everyone.

We'll talk very soon about the other kind of Marriage Blueprint, the Personal Marriage Blueprint, and you can see how we all work to "adjust" our beliefs on the basis of new information we have coming into our lives.

But first let's go back to miserable, depressed *James* and see if we can get him out of his depression. And then we'll return to work with your Personal Marriage Blueprint.

### Getting James "Un-Depressed"

Remember that James was constantly seeing bad stuff happening in his world and feeling more and more hopeless. Everything he was experiencing in his day had that flavor of pain and negativity to it.

I told him that it looked like he was leading a life driven by the following underlying belief system, and that the sooner he got over denying it the better. James believed:

- I'm at the age where death comes soon to men in my family.
- Because I'll die soon, nothing has much meaning.

- Other people are lazy and looking for a way out.
- There's really not much more in the world than bad news.
- All I do in life is struggle against the odds and try to be happy.
- People are always demanding things of me and are never satisfied.
- I'll never be happy or joyous, and what's the use anyway if I'm going to die soon.

Remember, he vigorously denied that this was what he thought or felt about himself and the world he was in, but that I said, "What you actually believe is demonstrated in what you do."

## The "undepression" experiment
## Try it yourself!

I asked him if he would do an experiment for a week or so that I felt strongly might help him become rapidly "undepressed." I said that he might consider it very strange or even crazy, but I have this belief that people can make radical changes in their lives, even become a totally different person in as little as only a few minutes.

I asked him how long he assumed it might take him to get "undepressed" through therapy. He answered that he expected it might take a year or two.

I responded, "If you think that it will take a year or two, that's your decision, of course. Personally, I would think it was pretty tiring and boring if it took me a year to get 'undepressed,' and I'd be kind of questioning the efficiency of that model of therapy."

He said he didn't see how it could take much less time, but wondered how much time I thought it should take to get "undepressed." I said what I always say to people when they ask about length of therapy.

**The actual changes only take maybe five minutes or so. People can make dramatic and extreme changes in only a matter of minutes.**

But it requires two things.

- The first is that they have a strong desire for the change. In other words, that there has to be at least 51% or more (preferably 80–90%) power in changing than in not changing.
- The second is that their Belief System allows for change.

Lots of people think they want to change something in their lives, but they never make much change of the kind they long for.

Remember, all Belief Systems scan for evidence to support their dominance and right to exist, especially Family Belief Systems. They are like animals that will bite off their legs to escape traps. They are powerful in their insistence on survival, and will not be denied.

They will do anything, including masquerading as something else.

So back to James. I asked him if he would be willing to do an experiment and that he didn't have to agree with me on anything, any principle or question I had about his Belief System. He only had to be very consistent in doing the experiment and we would check back in a week and see if anything had changed, in other words, if he felt less depressed.

## Take a Loaner! Borrow a Belief System!
## Cheaper Than a Rental Car,
## Same Price as a Library Book
## But Pays Like a Diamond Mine!

I told him I would give him a "loaner" of a Personal Belief System—he could borrow one of mine for a while and if he liked it, he could keep it. If he didn't like it he could always return to his old Belief System.

He clearly thought I was nuts, because he looked at me like I had just fallen out of the sky—after all, what could someone mean by loaning you a Belief System?

He said, OK, he would try the experiment, even though he couldn't see how it would do any good. I told him that the first part of the experiment was that he couldn't make such statements anymore during the next week. He agreed.

So here's the experiment:

"James, take these Beliefs along with you and **look for evidence** of the following:

- I am possibly an anomaly to the idea that men of my age die young, and possibly a new and interesting version of men in my family.
- Even if I died tomorrow, I want to be able to take my last breath saying "Wasn't yesterday as interesting as can be?"

- There's a ton of extremely interesting and varied people in the world, and I can't wait to talk to and understand all of their different ways of living and thinking and feeling. To that end, I'm going to start conversations with everyone I can by asking them an interesting question.
- There's definitely a lot of news going on in the world, but perhaps it's the harbinger of fascinating new developments that will bring unprecedented spiritual development in the world. You can't make omelets without breaking eggs. I wonder what the new omelet will be.
- Every day I have the resources to find some new way to make my life easier and more effective.
- People love me so much and respect me so much they can't wait to get my help and involvement in their lives. That's why my wife so frequently has new projects for me to do.
- Even if I die tomorrow, today I'm going to have as much fun as possible."

**I didn't ask him to accept any of these statements as "true,"** but just to think, feel, act and live according to them for a week as consistently and truly and honestly as he possibly could.

In other words, he was to do his best to "scan for evidence" in his world that every one of these statements was true.

**He was to try to "prove the truth" of these statements if only as an experiment.**

James accepted the terms of the experiment. How about you? You might say "yes" but would you be disciplined and honest about it, like he was?

I know when people start undermining the experiment within the first five minutes after giving it. They start to give me very clear reasons "why it won't work" for them. Their Family Belief System is "calling in backup" to destroy the "invader" before they even leave my office.

A great example, if very simple, is when people say "I'll *try it,* but I can't *promise* anything."

If you handed me a hundred dollar bill and asked me if I could hold it for you for five minutes while you go make a phone call, and I say "I'll try," would that inspire enough confidence in you to leave me with the hundred dollar bill?

I don't think so.

For some people, a pernicious Family Belief System will gather incredible strength anytime it is threatened, and will try to preserve itself against any new "intruder." A great example is found in some of the more orthodox and fundamentalist religious systems we have and the people involved in them. They simply will not even hear any new information, because their Belief System doesn't allow for new information. (It's considered, for example, satanic or heretical).

### My Spouse Is Not Who I Thought She Was!
### What's WRONG With Her?
### She's Gone Nuts!

It's for this reason also that some people have so much trouble in marriage to the point when they almost explode with hopelessness and helplessness. Many of us discover after marrying someone—somewhere down the line—that this person is "not who we thought they were," and the ensuing disappointment and pain can be quite severe!

In fact, what we have done most times is to picture them and their beliefs in our own image, and have never truly understood how different they are from us.

This is for the simple reason that very few people have any instruction or help in even knowing which questions to ask.

People come to counseling and therapy for a million reasons other than that they genuinely want change (at least in themselves). Many show up because they want change, in someone else!

For example, people come to marriage therapy as a way of demonstrating that they "have tried everything to make our marriage work, including therapy." But frequently they lack the genuine desire or drive to look at how they themselves are contributing to the "problems" in the marriage, and how they could or should change to create the outcomes they are seeking.

Fortunately, James said he would "do the experiment" and "give it a solid shot." He said that it was hard for him to see that it would do any good, but he now recognized that perhaps the reason this seemed hard to see was because he might have a preconceived idea of what he thought and believed.

I believed him, because he had already begun to see that he DID have this Family Belief System that he had denied only minutes earlier. I was pretty sure he would actually follow through. This meant that his own Personal Belief System was already beginning to change him.

If he would conscientiously follow this method for just a week, I knew he would begin to feel better and possibly even become "undepressed," the goal he expressed in the beginning of our session.

## I've seen countless miracles happen on these terms

When James began "evidence seeking" for the new Personal "loaner" Belief System, he quickly found plenty of evidence for these beliefs.

By the time he came to the next session, he said that he no longer felt depressed, but rather, energetic, excited, and that he was having fun in his daily life. I asked him why he didn't go ahead and cancel the session, in that case. He said that he suspected that the good effects would "wear off" and that he thought there "might be more to it," since that "seemed so simple and easy to do."

I assured him that change is often just that easy and that if he continued on this path for a while, he could easily stay "undepressed" or better yet, feeling great about his life for the rest of his life.

As a matter of fact, the new joyous and positive state of being might very quickly and powerfully become the "default" position in his life, such that if he were going to "try to be depressed," it would start to be hard to accomplish it!

Is change in therapy always that easy?

Not always. But it can be, and often is, when you are ready for that "five minute transformation," you are armed with the right information, and understand the effective steps to follow.

A lot of people for reasons of Family Belief Systems will insist on holding on to thoughts, feelings and beliefs that are against their own best interests for a long time despite understanding the power of changing Belief Systems.

Besides, sometimes it can take a little time to get practice in applying a new Belief System, so people may want to persist in the work for a while. The nice thing is that it's fun to do this work—for everyone, clients and therapists—because everyone is on the same track toward success and defined outcomes, and it's a matter of directed practice at that point.

In any case, James (like many other people) suddenly recognized something he never knew before, which was that he was capable of changing dramatically or very radically, and in a very short period of time.

This quick and dramatic change happened because of one thing: he recognized fully that his old Belief System was not serving him in the ways he would like, and that adopting a new Belief System produced dramatic results. He lowered his shield, and thought and felt differently and his whole way of experiencing the world changed instantly.

### Happy Call from James's Wife

I was working with him individually on this "depression" topic. But after the second session I had with him, his wife called me on the phone and said, "I don't know what you did to James, but whatever it was, do it some more and keep doing it. For the first time in our marriage, I have found him open to me, to the kids and to talking with pleasure about our future. I had actually been thinking about leaving him, since I could only picture a bleak future with him, even though he's a wonderful man and I love him. Now, I'm really looking forward to many more years with James. I sure hope this guy I'm seeing now is real and not just temporary."

### Love those kinds of calls! Makes my day!

Whether it is temporary or not depends on James and on what he decides to do with his new Belief System. It's clear that he immediately got different results within himself and with other people.

Whether he continues to keep the balance of power and energy on the new Personal Belief System or permits the "old friend" of his Family Belief System to reappear is up to him, and how he measures the results, and what he decides to do with these conclusions.

He might decide that it's just too uncomfortable to have an "undepressed" life, or might feel it's too unnatural or too "contrived" and revert to his old ways of seeing the world and himself in it. It can happen in an instant—just as fast as change happens in one direction, it can happen in the other direction—and he might just remain in his "depression-generating" Belief System.

### If He Can Do It, You Can Too!

The amazing thing about human beings is that we have personal choice and freedom always to decide how to respond to our circumstances. **Even in the most oppressive and horrible circumstances, we are still free to choose how to respond to those circumstances, and this will evolve from the Belief System we choose to follow.** An extraordinary and clear example of this is the book by Viktor Frankl, "Man's Search for Meaning," in which he describes the methods he used to give his life meaning and value, even to the time he spent in a Nazi concentration camp in World War II.

**If Viktor Frankl could do it in those circumstances, so can you in yours.** Yours CAN'T be that bad compared to his!

It might just be that you don't know you have a choice, however. James didn't know he had such a choice, or that it could make such a difference in his life, until I showed him the choice and spelled it out clearly to him.

The difference in his life (and the difference that can happen in yours, too) is that he now HAD **a choice** of the Belief System he would apply to his circumstances. He now recognized that he wasn't stuck with a single, solitary Belief System, but had a choice of the belief system he would use to drive his life.

# CHAPTER TWELVE

## Why I Claim Your Marriage Is *Already* Perfect!

If you remember back to the first chapter, I told Neal and Rita that their marriage is "the marriage they expect to have." Now I want to explain.

The title of this chapter might surprise you, but it is true. I'll explain what I mean. I want you to read this chapter very carefully and with the most open mind you can possibly have. Keep your defenses lowered!

*This is one of the most important, if not the most important idea I want you to understand in this whole book. And perhaps the most important thing you will ever hear in your whole life, and in particular in your married life.*

If you only get one thing out of this book, you need to understand and recognize the truth of this statement:

### The Marriage That You Have
### Is the Marriage You Expect to Have.

Consider the marriage that you have at this moment—not the one you might have one day or your fantasy of a good marriage. Not the marriage you think is possible or that you've heard others talk about or describe.

Your marriage right here, right now with both "warts and haloes"—that's what I want you to look at. Consider the following:

- The things you like and the things you do not like
- How you talk to each other, the style of talking, and words you use

- How you make love
- How often you make love
- The way you parent in general
- The way you parent boys
- The way you parent girls
- The way you interact with your extended families
- Your views of the conditions of marriage
- Your views about extramarital affairs
- Your views about saving money and spending money
- The ways you handle money in day to day budgeting
- How you are with friends and neighbors
- How you handle your need for togetherness
- How you handle your need for separateness and solitude
- Your reactions to one another
- How you handle conflict
- How you manage your religious life together
- Your statements about free time and how it should be spent
- The way you work together around the house
- The way you see your partner in relation to you
- The way you see yourself as a partner
- The way you see men in marriage
- The way you see women in marriage
- Your views about who should work and how and how much
- Your feelings about children in the house
- Your views about children and their education
- Your views about your family and mixing with other ethnicities
- Your views about retirement
- Your views about what your wedding vows meant
- Your views about handling illness, individually and as a family

## The Marriage That You Have
## Is the Marriage You Expect to Have

All of the things you noted as "currently happening" in your marriage actually do reflect your expectations.

Re-consider the case of James who, by the terms of his "depression-generating" Belief System, was expecting to find things in the world which were negative, painful and disappointing, and thus he DID find those things And thus his depression-generating Belief System indeed did create a state of depression in his life.

In other words, the world he carried inside became the world he expressed on the outside. Further, not only did he create a depression and a depressing world for himself, but he created a feeling of disappointment, disillusionment and pain for his wife and children.

They felt and experienced the world he created, even though that world only generated from his own beliefs and not from the world as it was. Remember, that which the world generates is only data, information, and that data is neutral until we assign it meaning: good, bad, positive or negative.

The same goes for your marriage.

**The marriage you have, the one you are living right now, is the perfect reflection of the one you expect to have.**

What people think about a marriage that is having problems is usually exactly the opposite of what you are reading here. They think that their view of the marriage they expect to have is just road-blocked by circumstances, for example, that their spouse is being difficult, or because they don't have money or "do" certain things.

### PLEASE, No "If Only's"

Most people in strained marriages imagine, "If only_____, then everything would be right."

"If only my husband were kinder then everything would be all right."

"If only we went to church then everything would be right."

"If only my wife would give me more sex then everything would be right."

"If only our kids were grown up then everything would be right."

"If only we had more money then everything would be right."

This kind of thinking will only make you more miserable and won't solve the problems. Only changing your belief system will.

I've seen a large number of couples who came to therapy **after they had "solved" these problems, and they found out that they still didn't have a satisfying and joyous marriage.**

I'm not denying that there can be "external" problems.

It's true that many times, in many circumstances a lack of enough money, sex, kindness, spiritual direction, or difficult kids can cause strains in a marriage.

However, it's also true that many marriages have one or even all these "problems," and they STILL have a Great Marriage, as you remember in the story of Rick and Donna.

**The "problems" in a marriage are not "out there." The conflicts are "inside you."**

Whatever you might be thinking of as "problems," or unsatisfying results in your marriage (or other part of your life, for that matter: money issues, free time, doing the work you want to do, friendships, parenting or anything else) is just the reflection of your already existing expectations.

In case that slipped by you, let me say it again.

**What you consider "problems" in your life are what you already expect to happen in your life.**

Said another way, what you think of as "problems" in your life are actually "solutions" that fit the Belief System you are operating out of.

These "solutions" might feel very uncomfortable to you, but they are the solutions you have come up with to reflect the expectations you already have.

### How do you feel about it?
### Did you create your situation?
### Is your life as it is a direct choice of yours?
### Is it true or false?

- If you are poor, it is because you expect to be poor.
- If you are angry, it is because you expect to be angry.
- If you are a victim, it is because you expect to be a victim.
- If you are sad, it is because you expect to be sad.
- If you are happy, it is because you expect to be happy.
- If you are sick, it is (to a certain extent) because you expect to be sick.
- If you are well, it is (to a large degree) because you expect to be well.
- If you are rich, it is because you expect to be rich.

- If you are successful at business, it is because you expect success.
- If you are a wonderful sex partner, it's because you expect to be a wonderful sex partner.
- If you are disappointed in the sex you get, it's because you expect to be disappointed in the sex you get.
- If you are thrilled with your sex life, it's because you expect to be thrilled with your sex life.
- If you are late to appointments, it's because you expect to be late to appointments.
- If you procrastinate, it's because you expect to procrastinate.
- If you do things on time, it's because you expect to do things on time.
- If you learn things quickly, it's because you expect to learn things quickly.
- If you learn things slowly, it's because you expect to learn things slowly.
- If you have a satisfying marriage, it's because you expect to have a satisfying marriage.
- If you have an unsatisfying marriage, it's because you expect to have an unsatisfying marriage.

When I say that you "expect to have an unsatisfying marriage," that might sound completely insane to you. Why would you expect dissatisfaction? You wouldn't consciously or deliberately.

I don't know anyone who would say, "I think I'll get married because I expect dissatisfaction from the experience."

Yet people—well over half of them and maybe as much as 75% of Americans—are from a little to very dissatisfied with their marriages.

How did that happen? Something was working in the background. That something is the Belief System that accompanies their view of marriage (your Marriage Blueprint).

A lot can go wrong when you get intimate with another person. One of the things that can go wrong is that you have misread the person— or misread yourself.

You might have one model of marriage, and your partner might have a very opposite one.

And you might not have even noticed.

As human beings, we have this pernicious tendency. *We tend to think other people are (or even that they should be) like us.*

Or if they aren't like us, eventually they will be like us after enough exposure to us (when they see the light of how right we are in the ways we think, feel and believe about things).

Problem is that the other person is doing the same thing.

## And people don't like to be told how to be.

People are like big trucks running downhill on mountain highways. They tend to keep going in the same direction with a lot of momentum unless and until something even bigger (such as a bridge or a giant boulder or another truck) gets in the way and then it tends to be a big crash.

What most of us DON'T know when we make our marriage vows.

- We don't expect our spouse to have a very different model of marriage than we do—we don't usually know there are different models of marriage!
- We just assume that everybody has the same models after all, don't most people take essentially the same "Vows?"
- We expect that after a long enough period of time, we will "rub off" on the other person, and that they will see things "our way" (it doesn't happen).
- We think that we'll "cross that bridge—**conflict**—when we get there." But *when we get to the bridge,* we don't know how to get across it because no one has taught us.
- We have **no idea what our actual model of marriage is**
- We often end up feeling extremely disappointed when marriage isn't like the marriage manuals say it should be

## The marriage that you have is
## The marriage that you expect to have.

In other words, if your marriage is harmonious, wonderful, smooth, loving, warm and easy, it's not just because you and your spouse are wonderful people (of course you are, but that's beside the point), but also because you have some agreement on Family Belief Systems and Family Marriage Blueprints.

How did you know that before you got married? Well, some people seem to know these things. But most of us don't.

Sometimes it happens that people who come from very similar religious backgrounds, or very similar neighborhoods or ethnicities, get married and are "instantly compatible."

## Arranged Marriages Were More Successful!
## Why?

Studies have demonstrated that "arranged marriages" where the parents decide far in advance who should marry whom, often work very well and people frequently have a powerful sense of wellbeing and satisfaction in these marriages.

Being "free to choose anyone you want" hasn't always worked out for everyone. Previous cultures with traditions of marrying in more prescribed ways had "built-in" Blueprints about marriage which, while they didn't meet everyone's ultimate desires, often were able to make extremely good matches.

## "Community Compatibility"

*"Matchmakers"* in certain traditions also were people who had lots of connections, lots of understanding about people, and often uncanny or extremely intuitive knowledge about how to join individuals, families and groups. They had "street smarts" about this that modern "compatibility tests" can never match.

But for most of us, it seems pretty much like a "crap shoot" how our marriage is going to turn out.

# CHAPTER THIRTEEN

# "Honey, I Shrunk the Marriage"

The strongest measure of whether a marriage will last, and be a happy one, is the way the couple handles disillusionment. Sooner or later, you are going to feel disappointed and disillusioned in your married life.

Disillusionment is the experience of having a positive expectation and then feeling deeply disappointed—and it's going to happen to you if it hasn't yet.

It's well known that most marriages have "honeymoon" periods at the beginning. In this "honeymoon phase," it seems that everything goes smoothly and everybody just basks in love, tolerance and joy. You revel in the experience of being joined together. The grass is greener, the sky is bluer, people are wonderful, and life itself is wonderful.

## The BIG WORLD you start out with

Take your arms and spread them out as far as you can, like a little kid does when he or she is talking about something they think of as huge, and they say, "It's THIS big!" That's the way a kid has of saying "it's as big as anything can possibly be!"

Say you meet someone and fall in love.

You have a very large picture of the universe of possibilities at this first, glorious time of getting to know one another. It seems that anything is possible. At the beginning of your relationship, your world together is so big, so alive, that it seems that nothing can bring it down or shrink it.

You feel you can talk with this person about everything, and that you are totally interested in everything your partner has to say to you. Open, huge, almost infinite!

It seems like nothing can come along to take anything from you. What a wonderful state of being!

### Then you SHRINK the world

*Then one day,* after expressing your undying love to one another, you are talking about something openly and without defenses, and one of you *brings up something* (say, previous sexual experiences or budgeting or having children), and the *other one bristles a bit over the comment and it clearly hurts or bothers them.*

The next time you or your lover is about to bring up this "delicate subject," you'll be a tiny bit more careful not to step on one another's toes.

You'll edit your comments a little more, and be more conscientious and hesitant about how you discuss the issue.

Or maybe you'll even stop bringing it up.

*Didn't that "BIG" world just shrink a bit?*

It got a little smaller just then, didn't it?

And the process goes on.

You chip off one little piece of your "big world" at a time, until, after a while, the world you are living in (within your marriage) has become small, almost infinitesimal, and even strangling or claustrophobic.

### Rule of Law Shrinks Your World and Your Marriage

So it becomes a Rule of Law that certain topics, statements, actions, ways of speaking, words, manners of dress, sexual conduct, spiritual ideas, religious expectations, political expectations, family traditions, family expectations, views about money, parenting and neighbors, etc. etc. will now be applied to your relationship because you have become subject to the "laws of marriage."

This engine of "law" immediately begins to take effect, and all sorts of "rules" and expectations begin to enter into the relationship. Unspoken "contracts" are being signed left and right, about how you are to conduct yourself sexually, whether and how you are to have contact with others, how you are to treat members of the family, how money is to be managed between you, and who is to pay for what, and on and on.

---

What the heck just happened?

Lots of contracts are being agreed to without being fully discussed.

## How to Write the Future, a Different One

We start "writing the future" with potential spouses the minute we meet them. On the one hand that's a wonderful ability of human beings, the talent of imagining the future and picturing yourself and the other person in that picture.

I often say to people, *"Looks like you wrote the whole movie already!"* This is because in lots of couples' relationships (as in every other part of life), it's tempting to begin to plan and mentally expect all kinds of things in one's future, some of which might be realistic and probable, and others which might be very unlikely.

It's a natural tendency and even a wonderful thing to project and plan the future. However, one thing that happens is that one of you might be writing "one movie," and the other one might be writing a completely different one. Happens all the time.

And it can be a rude awakening to find out that you are in someone else's movie, and no too happy about it.

## How To Over-Adapt; You Don't Want To Do This!

A woman might say, "I would love to have a career and my own personal life—we could travel a lot—and maybe not have children for a long time," when her Family Marriage Blueprint absolutely calls for children right away.

She's adopted this view, and possibly her husband will think he's found that "one gem of a woman," who actually thinks about marriage like he does. **He's going to be in for a rude surprise.**

A man might say, "I really love the part of intimacy that comes with having someone there every day, really getting to know me—it's what I really long for in marriage," when in fact his Family Marriage Blueprint calls for him to be away at work making a large income and being the sole provider for the family ("men do that," he feels)—and the majority of his life will be spent at the office.

He's adopted another vision, and in some sense is **selling it to her.** He truly believes the adopted version at the moment, but he's not going to live that way, ultimately. His wife is going to be power-fully disappointed if she accepts and thinks that he's going to live by that movie.

### Secret and "Unspoken" Contracts
### You Don't Know You Are Signing!
### The Small Print Is Invisible!

We just don't *know in advance* the hidden and secret contracts we are signing when we get into marriage or intimate relationships! Furthermore, one doesn't even have to be in an engagement or formally declared committed relationship for this "movie writing" and "contract signing" activity to get launched.

Almost everyone begins to create the contracts at the slightest implication of a committed relationship. **We are born movie script writers and contract makers.** The combination of imagination of the future together, and creation of rules about what you expect in this future from a partner, is an automatic process that is unstoppable.

The most you can do is be aware of its going on. It always goes on in one way or another, and by the time I've described all the components of the Marriage Blueprints, you'll see the how and the why of the entire process.

### Basically, we are always trying to get reality around us
### to conform to our expectations, and be what we want it
### to be, and how we want it to be.

This is part of that "scanning the environment" and "evidence-seeking" I spoke about. Our Belief Systems are constantly seeking confirmation of our conclusions, thoughts and feelings about things in our world. If we believe others are reliable and trustworthy, we'll (our Belief System will) always be looking for evidence of that, and simultaneously pressuring or manipulating people around us to be both reliable and trustworthy. We really want the world to be like we expect it to be!

If we believe that others are unreliable and untrustworthy, we'll (Our Belief System will) always be scanning for evidence of that, and simultaneously pressuring or manipulating people around us to be examples of unreliability and untrustworthiness.

**You are always trying to get the world to conform to your expectations.** Whether you know it or not, it's going on all the time. It's just the process that happens, and it's one of those ways of solution-seeking our mind engages in.

It's how we survive and keep interested in our world.

## Sorting and Scanning
## For Your Future Spouse

So, if you meet a new person today that you feel attracted to, and that person seems like a potential partner or even faintly like a potential marriage partner, even today and even this minute, the Evidence-Seeking Machine that is your Belief System will be scanning for verification of this being a good choice.

You'll start scanning for reasons that this person *would or would not* qualify as a marriage partner. You won't necessarily recognize the process occurring. On a strictly conscious level, you might just be thinking "what a nice person, someone nice to hang out with," or something just as innocuous.

But your Marriage Blueprint Belief System will be generating all kinds of judgments and conclusions about this person. Good potential spouse? Bad potential spouse? What would it be like?

Will this person be right in the movie script I have written for them and me? Or will they disappoint me? What if I get hurt? What if I end up not liking this person? What if he or she is not what they appear to be?

You "pre-marry" every person who is a candidate and test it out in your own mind according to how you think that it will go for you.

Most of the time, our spouses don't follow the scripts we write for them in just the way we wrote the movie! It's disappointing.

At first, Jenny's husband was doing everything she always hoped a man would do. He was giving her Valentine's Day cards, surprising her with flowers, calling to see how she was doing during the day, having long talks with her into the night about everything under the sun. But after about a year, things began to change.

Todd (her husband) forgot to get flowers. Then he stopped calling during the day, stopped setting up dates, and she started to ask,

"Does he still love me?" To her, it didn't seem like it. It seemed like he had lost interest. Had he? It's hard to know without talking to Todd, isn't it?

According to Todd, he loved her even more than he ever had since the day they met. But he had started to focus on showing that love through working harder and longer hours so they could have a house of their own.

# CHAPTER FOURTEEN

## How You Got a Bad Reputation with Your Spouse; What Can You Do?

## ("Honey, If You Could Start All Over, Would You Marry Me Again?")

From the first time you meet someone, you start creating an "image" of that person. You carry this image of them, like a picture in a locket around your neck. You then view the person as the same as that image. Trouble is, images stay the same, but people change!

Remember the first time you met your sweetheart? Remember what she (he) looked like, how she smelled, how hopeful you were that you would be together? Remember how wonderful she seemed, unlike any other person you've ever met? Seemingly heaven sent, just the right person for you like no one else could ever be? Now how do you see that very same person? Did she change, or did something else happen?

You think that this "image" of them is based on their behavior, and how they act toward you, toward themselves and toward others. But more than that, you create an image of that person which may or may not bear much similarity to who they actually are! You might convince yourself that the person is "kind at heart," when all of your friends clearly see that he is a jerk! You might think that he is tough and steady when others see that he is "flighty" and very unreliable.

The "image" of another person we meet is always based on our own Belief System. This belief system process can create images or "fantasies" out of any person or situation that will fit our hopes and belief. Remember that parched people lost in a desert begin to see visions of "oasis," when nothing is really there—based on their need for water!

Remember I said that we (and our cherished Belief Systems) are always looking for "evidence" and that we are "evidence-seeking mechanisms?"

And remember I said that we are always evaluating ourselves and others according to those Beliefs (Family and Personal)?

And remember I said that we are always trying to get reality to conform to the Belief Systems we already have?

When we create our "image" of another person, it will always be formed on the basis of this process.

In some ways, every other human being is to us only a "player in our own play." I don't mean that in any negative or demeaning way, or to suggest that you don't take other people seriously, or as important in their own right!

If you remember Todd from the last chapter, he was Jenny's "ideal man" when they first got together. He was doing everything Jenny always dreamed a man would do for her. But then he stopped doing those things. Jenny had "frozen" this initial picture of Todd as the one she cherished. And when he stopped acting the way she wanted him to, she felt betrayed.

## We can never truly know another person,
## Only our image of that other person
### Good News or Bad News?

We can never know another person but only our **image of that other person**. We can only know them through the filter of our own Beliefs. It's certainly true that really honest, genuine and expressive people together can gain a great deal more information and true image of one another than we do with strangers.

Jenny's image of a husband and lover was not getting updated. She felt like he had abandoned her and didn't love her anymore! But Todd had only begun to focus more on his own view of what a true expression of love is all about—to create financial security for their family.

There's a disconnect between Todd and Jenny and their "ideals" of marriage. If they continue with this disconnect for very long, it will begin to seem to them that they "don't even know each other anymore!"

People can live together very closely, and seemingly very intimately, for 50 years or more in marriage or other relationships, and in reality may have very little understanding of who that person is outside of the filters through which they are seen.

I've met with couples where it's just plain obvious that neither one truly took the time to update their information on who the other person is after years of being together. They still held the same image, expectations, views and opinions about one another which they had 30 or more years ago.

### Living together for even a very long time is no guarantee whatsoever that people will truly know each other

Living together for even a very, very long time is no guarantee whatsoever that people will actually know each other as they truly are, or any better than they did in the first ten minutes they met.

Sure, you might know the other person's habits and expressed likes and dislikes very well. You might be able to describe in incredible detail a lot of things about your partner, but, in truth, you might be extremely "off" in some of the most important aspects of who that person is at their core.

How odd to be married to someone for 50 years, and ultimately find out that you don't know that person at all. But I can assure you it happens quite a lot more often than you would think.

And, of course, the other thing that happens, as I said before, is that people change, sometimes extremely rapidly and sometimes very dramatically and spectacularly, from one period of their life to another.

Elizabeth, a wonderful woman of 81 years of age, had waited for many decades to be able to travel, her deep passion in life. She had waited for her children to get grown and independent before she could do extensive traveling. Tragically, her youngest daughter and husband died in a car wreck. Elizabeth happily raised the grandchildren, but had put off her own passion.

Finally the grandchildren were grown and on their own, and Elizabeth began to arrange the travels she had so longed to take. She had saved very diligently and was now ready to hit the road!

Her husband Roberto hates travel! He considers it a complete waste of time and money. He thought she had "come to her senses" over the years and given up on the folly of traveling—even though Elizabeth subscribed to travel magazines and talked about "one of these days" for many decades. It was as if Roberto had "gone deaf" to this part of Elizabeth.

Now that the time had come, and Elizabeth was literally buying tickets and preparing to travel—and inviting Roberto to come along—she and her husband entered into the deepest conflict and most painful time of their whole marriage of 55 years.

Elizabeth always hoped that Roberto would "soften up" as he grew older and see the wonderful value of traveling. Roberto always hoped Elizabeth would "come to her senses."

It's a real problem, and even after all these years of marriage, this issue may end up splitting them apart.

## You Are "Writing Parts" In Your "Personal Movie" For Other People You Meet

As I said, from the beginning that you meet someone, you very quickly (or even instantly) develop an image of who that person is—a conclusion about them. It's usually quite profound and strong, and very often never changes.

This is both fortunate and unfortunate.

Fortunate, since we can feel powerful attraction and connection to someone this way.

Unfortunate, since we tend to "lock someone in" to an image of who we think they are, and begin to create all kinds of expectations of them from that moment on (sometimes for the rest of their lives and ours).

Then begins the really insidious and complicated process of "reputation."

In the case of Elizabeth and Roberto, Elizabeth views Roberto as "stuck and stubborn in his little life and a much smaller person than I ever thought he would be," and Roberto views Elizabeth as "not the sensible person I thought she was at all, but rather a wasteful and flighty woman."

### Does Your Spouse Have a *Good Reputation* Or A *Bad Reputation* with You?

In relationships, as I said, we start by creating an image of who another person is, what they stand for, what they are capable of, who we feel they will be in relation to us and other people, what they believe and how they act, and a million other things established by each of us in the blink of an eye when we meet someone.

And as I said, this "image" arises from our Belief System.

We are looking for people to be "evidence" of our Belief System and represent something to us in our life. We don't want to be alone, and we want to feel that life has meaning. We try to find someone who will conform to our own beliefs of what a spouse should be and how they should act. If we find that person, we think, they will be the "right one" for us!

### Jane's View of Marriage And How Cal "Betrayed" Her (He didn't)

My friend Jane believes that marriages exist so people can truly support and protect each other in a difficult and rather dangerous world. She sees the world as a dangerous place, and has a strong reliance on her husband to provide a lot of her sense of security and peace in the world.

As I've said many times before there's nothing good or bad about this or any other Belief System. It's about whether it serves you, and results in what you most cherish and value.

In Jane's case, because she has those views about marriage and the world, she was always looking for a husband who would "be there for her" in all kinds of conditions, and with whom, in her words, she would "never feel abandoned."

### This Is Different from Cal's View of Marriage

She married Cal in part because she saw him as strong, secure and consistent. He's a big, tenderhearted guy with an inviting smile and incredible warmth. I see how she could easily conclude about him that he would certainly "fit the spot" of a husband for her.

That was her "image" of Cal: strong, secure and consistent.

Is he those things? In some ways, yes.

Did she "invent him in her mind" as an answer to her Marriage Blueprint?

Most definitely.

How is he "doing" in fulfilling this "image?"

Well, sometimes not so well.

## Often Cal Would Rather Be Hunting and Fishing. Uh-Oh!

You see, Cal is a very dedicated and passionate hunter and fisherman. He loves going into the mountains to hunt for elk and on backcountry expeditions to pursue fish. He likes to be gone a lot.

So, in addition to the "image" that Jane has of Cal, he also now has a "reputation" with her.

His "reputation" is that he's not completely reliable, and that he sometimes is perfectly capable of "betraying" and "abandoning" her—even though in actual fact he is doing nothing of the sort, according to him!

Cal is perfectly aware of this "reputation" that he constantly has to contend with in his marriage with Jane. Sometimes it doesn't make him very happy, as a matter of fact, he kind of gets "riled up" at her.

Why?

## But What is JANE'S Reputation?

Well, Cal had an image of Jane from the beginning too!

He saw Jane as one of the most self-sufficient women he had met. She had a great job with her own paralegal office. She had lived on her own for a long time and bought her own house, car and had several employees whom she managed very well.

She seemed to have very strong and honest opinions on all kinds of things, and was a brilliant and very intelligent thinker.

He really liked that about her and felt very drawn to her, in part, on the basis of those qualities.

His Belief System and Marriage Blueprint called for two married people to be strong and independent and have their own independent interests and life, while being together in a committed relationship.

He "never liked clingy, whiny women," in his words.

His image of Jane was that she was NOT one of those women, but in fact very self-sufficient.

So now, her "reputation" with him, based on the fact that she feels hurt and abandoned when he goes fishing and hunting (just pursuing his own personal interests!), is tarnished.

### Disappointment in Your "Image" of Your
### Spouse and How You React To This Disappointment
### Determines The Future Of Your Marriage!

He has a lesser "opinion" of her than when they met, and she has a worse "reputation" than she used to with him.

This is how it works.

- **Image first,** which is a spontaneous "fitting" of the person (in your imagination and completely based on fantasy and intuition) to your Belief System and Marriage Blueprint.
- Then based on the person's behavior and their "conformity" to your expectations and image of them (or lack of conformity), **they begin to have a "reputation" with you.**

Do you see that a person's reputation with you (your opinion and thought of them) doesn't have a whole lot to do with what they do, but the degree they conform to your expectations and "image" of them?

To some women, Cal's going hunting and fishing would certainly not only be acceptable, but something they would strongly encourage and feel good about (based on their own Marriage Blueprint and Belief System). And to some women, his combination of strength and consistency with his personal interests and desire to have his own life would make him seem like a wonderfully balanced person.

To those women, with a different image and expectation set, Cal would have a "good reputation."

To some men, Jane's combination of her own self-sufficiency and independent thinking with her strong belief about marriage being about consistent closeness and intimacy would be extremely appealing. And to some men, that combination would seem very much like the elements of a wonderfully balanced person.

To those men, with a different image and expectation set, Jane would have a "good reputation."

> ## So you see, the primary relationship and the marriage ALWAYS *begins in the head.*
> ## *Not in the heart.*

People who say they "think with their heart" don't have much understanding of what is happening.

It's all part of our efforts to "evidence-gather," to do our best to find evidence that the world is as we imagine or believe it to be.

Our Belief System will not really allow us to proceed in any other way.

Here's the important part of this.

**You and every other person on the planet (including me) go around with a whole set of Beliefs and Blueprints against which we are constantly measuring the world, in terms of its conformity to these expectations.**

We are gathering evidence for the Belief Systems we have. Why? Because we want to prove that world is how we think it is, so we'll feel good, comfortable, right, justified, and have a sense of meaning in our world.

*And which of us is right?*

We all are.

> ## Every single Belief System ever invented is right and wrong at the same time.

Every single culture ever invented is right and wrong at the same time.

Every single religion, form of spirituality, worship and view of the universe that has ever been invented is right and wrong at the same time.

### Your Family Belief Blueprint knows all the answers—for you!

If you don't think I'm right, just ask yourself a question about anything, such as whether there is a loving, personal God who cares for you and me; and you DO have a ready answer, even if the answer is, "I don't know and no one else does either."

That may very well be your Personal or "learned" Belief Blueprint, or it might be the one you first established as a child, I couldn't know that.

But you do have answers inside, and some part of you is completely, totally, and unchangeably certain of those answers!

Why is this important to know?

- It's important so you understand **why you get angry, frustrated, hurt, betrayed and insulted by other people.**
- It's important so you **recognize the source of that hurt**—and can see that the source of that hurt is really not in the other person, but in your own beliefs and expectations, image and "reputation" expectations of the other person.
- It's important so you can be **free of the traps** you have gotten into in your marriage or long-term relationships, where you end up feeling confused and frustrated and saying things like "I thought I knew him/her" and "I never saw this coming."

### Understand That You Never Really Know Anyone.

You never know anyone fully. You only know the "image" you have of them.

There are billions of other people in the world who are so radically different from you, and have such dramatically different Belief Systems and Marriage Blueprints than you, that it would completely spin your head around if you truly grasped it.

### So you have two jobs:

1. Know that you **have a Belief System driving every thought, feeling and action you do whether you know it or not,** and that you have no obligation to change your Belief System one bit. It's just as valid as the next person's by 100%, and

2. Know that other people in the world might share some fragment of your Beliefs, but they might not, too—and **they are under no obligation whatsoever to be your image of who they are, or to conform to your expectations that they be who you want them to be. You are not the ruler even of your own universe, let alone theirs.**

Sound familiar? It's the Intimacy Paradox, right? 100% acceptance of yourself and 100% acceptance of others.

Implementing these "two jobs" described above will help you get a strong feeling of freedom and taking pure responsibility (and credit) for your life. It's quite impossible to make much progress or get much success in life until you have done this.

That leads us to the next step.

*Now it's time for us you to discover the Personal Marriage Blueprint,* how you create it and what it means to you—and how it is different from your Family Marriage Blueprint.

# CHAPTER FIFTEEN

## Construct Your Own Personal Marriage Blueprint

As you grow and develop in understanding from childhood into adulthood, new influences come in to your life. New thoughts, new ideals, new relationships with people who may be far different from you, and who bring unexpected changes in the ways you always thought people "were," and how marriages and families were "supposed to be."

- As a kid, you see models of marriage before you, such as those exhibited by your parents, an extended family of adults, neighbors, movies and television family personalities, and perhaps even instruction at church, temple or mosque, and perhaps some other influences, such as those of your parents.
- And remember, you are constantly (and almost completely unconsciously, at least early on) making conclusions about marriage based on how you feel and interpret what you see.
- Mostly, you are simply receiving the instructions embedded in your parents' and other adults' models of marriage.

Remember the two kids I talked about who had totally different reactions to their parents? One thought that the parents were always fighting, never getting along, that the mother was totally controlling and the father was hen-pecked; and the other admired their parents as very lively, dynamic people and who admired her father for his openness to the mother and the mother for being strong and independent?

Same parents, different conclusions!

As I said before, these conclusions based on observations and direct experience represent the strongest and earliest form of Marriage Blueprint we create.

Although we are not thinking about it in detail as kids, this original or Family Marriage Blueprint contains a lot of information which influences the way we see all kinds of things later in life.

### The "Ingredients" in Your Personal Marriage Blueprint

For example:

- How you handle differences of opinion in marriage
- How men and women are in marriage
- How the topics of money, free time, parenting and other things are handled in marriage

Both brother and sister have their own conclusions, but the same "environment," that is to say, their parents' marriage, influences them both.

Early in life, even though we are thinking humans, our ability to access much more than our own emotional reactions is very low.

Most of these conclusions and perspectives are based on emotional or "physical" reactions to their parents' interactions—how it "feels" to them.

### It's Not Your Parents' Fault.
### It's Not Your Fault.
### It's NOBODY'S Fault.

And remember what I said before, that what you conclude is not "your parents' fault!" It's **your conclusions** based on data and information that is neutral, even though it sure doesn't feel like it at the time!

It's just the way it is!

This is so primary to our experience that it tends to influence everything we think, feel and believe later.

Because our early conclusions in our lives are so strongly based on primary systems of our body and our emotional reactions—the physical responses of fear, happiness, excitement, anger and sadness and the impact of these on us—it continues to feel into adult life like our views are very true and logical.

We take these early experiences, and our emotional and physical reactions to them, as some kind of golden truth or certainty, when in fact, they are the immature, simple, and almost sheer "animal responses" we have to the neutral data and information coming at us.

### Here Are Some Remembrances of People
### Who Recall Making Decisions About
### What Kind of Marriage They Would Have →
### Which Lead To Conclusions →
### Which Lead To Beliefs →
### Which Lead to Creating Their Marriage Blueprint →
### Which Leads to How They Think, Feel and Act
### About Marriage →
### Which Leads to What Kind of Marriage They Have →

Any of these sound familiar to you?

"I decided right then and there that I'd never let a man treat me like my dad treated my mother" (**Sylvia,** remembering a decision made at age 8).

"My mother had told me so many lies by then, and my father had always been so truthful with me, that I started to feel like women were liars and men were the ones that could be trusted" (**Jasmine** remembering being 10 years old).

"Whenever we kids did something bad, my parents just got really quiet and didn't say a thing, but the tension was so thick you could cut it with a knife. I remember just wishing that someone would say something, or that I could just get a spanking and get it over with. It was horrible, and I thought I would never treat my kids like that when I grew up" (**Ted** remembering being 12 years old).

"My dad and mom were always playing pranks on each other, like my mom putting cayenne pepper in my dad's underpants, or my dad who went to a shop and bought some glasses which looked just like my mom's, but which were a totally different prescription; and seeing the look on her face when she put them on. It looked like it was going to be a lot of fun to be an adult, and I couldn't wait. And I hoped I would get a wife as funny as my mother" (**Jimmy** remembering being 9 years old).

"It seemed like all my parents ever did was read books and listen to music. I always wanted to go places, camping or to the show or somewhere, and I remember thinking it must be awfully boring, or you must get to be a boring person as soon as you get to be an adult" (**Katie** remembering being 9 years old).

And of course, these are consciously and deliberately remembered conclusions—but they are definitely decisions that kids make all the time!

## You made conclusions about marriage as a kid
## Whether you remember them or not!

Most of us have a whole raft of such conclusions that are either partially conscious or almost completely unconscious, and yet they have a powerful and permanent effect on our Belief Systems and our Marriage Blueprint.

This early or Family Marriage Blueprint develops in each and every one of us, no matter what situation we are in. The human mind is a "solution machine," and is always taking in the available data and making conclusions and ideas, which we then combine with feelings to create beliefs.

## We make conclusions from our circumstances.
## These conclusions form beliefs

**And then we live by those beliefs.**

We think, feel, and act based on those beliefs.

Even more extraordinary is the fact that we even see reality through the filters of those beliefs, as I showed you in the story of James and his "undepression" process.

We see what our Belief Systems allow us to see.

We don't see what our Belief System doesn't allow us to see.

The Jesuits used to say that if they got a child before 6 years old they could assure his training and faith, but after that, it got harder and harder.

Quite true.

## The 9 Year Old "Old Man"

The Family Belief System is actually established by around 9 years of age, based on the accumulation of data and conclusions that have been made by then. It is based on the fact that kids by that age have developed enough of an ability to problem solve, and make their own decisions, that they can clearly create a Primary or Family Belief System.

They can handle a rudimentary understanding, for example, of what a marriage is. They can tell you a lot about their parents' relationship, how they get along, what they talk about, what their parents' opinions are on a broad variety of topics. And whether they are affectionate, whether they sleep in the same bed (and they can give you a theory about why not, if they don't), whether they "love each other," and a variety of other fairly complicated concepts about the adult world.

But, of course, their version and understanding of those things is still quite primitive and simple, but **exceedingly powerful!**

By this, I mean that the Belief System they have established by that age, including their opinions on marriage and adulthood, is now a permanent FACT of their life, and all new information they receive will be continuously and persistently filtered through those systems.

So how important is parental influence in kids establishing their own Family Marriage Blueprint?

Pretty important—but not the only influence.

As I have said, each person will actually create his or her own set of beliefs from their conclusions about the data. However, parents can also be very helpful to their children in aiding them in this process.

Most parents are the opposite of helpful in this arena.

For example, they say they love each other to the kids, but say a lot of hateful, spiteful and insulting things to one another.

That's going to have an impact.

### *Making Marriage Decisions, Beginning At Age 9*

And yet a lot of kids will be able to experience intuitively or instinctively that the parents perhaps really do love each other.

And, after all is said and done, each kid cares most about whether he or she is loved, understood and respected, just like every single person on the planet, and as long as he or she feels those things, there's a sense of freedom inside to think and feel about everything else.

But *every kid still creates a Marriage Blueprint spontaneously* based on their conclusions about what parents do, and if there's a ton of negativity, coldness, hurt and disrespect, any child is going to develop a pretty aversive Family Marriage Blueprint!

**By age 9 and above (it varies from kid to kid somewhat), every kid can give answers to all these questions**

- Do you think you'll get married?
- At what age do you think you'll get married?
- Will you have children?
- How many? How many boys and how many girls?
- Does it look like fun being grown up and married and a parent?
- What do you think will be the most fun about being grown up and married and having kids of your own?
- What do you think will be the hardest thing about being grown up and married and having kids of your own?
- What kind of (mother/father) do you think you'll be?
- What do you think your (wife/husband) will be like?
- Will your (husband/wife) be like your (father/mother) or different?

And other such questions.

They won't have any trouble answering these questions.

When kids are thinking about something that pleases them and that they enjoy, they rarely have any problem telling you about it.

When it's uncomfortable, they are just like we adults. They start getting "defensive" in the few ways they have developed at that point—get silent and look away, try to distract you from the question, get upset at you for asking the question. Like I said, just like we adults!

What did **you** decide about marriage at age 9?

## A Little Older, Then Off to "Marriage Boot Camp"

Just like summer camp, but summer camp you can forget! This kind of "marriage boot camp" you remember vividly!

As time goes on and you get a little older, beginning around 12 years of age or so, you start feeling a little more pressure about the "marriage" question. Some of the kids start pairing off, and talk about being boyfriends and girlfriends.

"Sherry likes Dan!" they start whispering. "But Dan likes Jennifer."

"No! Jennifer hates *him,* but she is crazy about David!"

If you don't go pair yourself off, there are plenty of people around at this age very willing to do it for you! Because the game starts, everyone starts playing at pairing, looking in a mostly very innocent way at the future, at being married to someone else.

### This is when you start practicing at being married

Remember, I said that people don't have to be anywhere near in a committed relationship before they begin "writing and scripting the movie" of their marriage?

This starts happening very early.

Of course, it seems benign and simple minded enough—and even "cute" that they are engaged in "puppy love"—*but it's pretty deadly serious when you are in the middle of it.*

Kids already know that they are starting Marriage Boot Camp—not consciously of course, but in some part of their being it's quite clear. Their successes and failures based on their Belief Systems with other people in this "practice marriage" feels very consequential to them.

They have years of observation, processing data and concluding all kinds of things about marriage and adult life. More years than people spend in college and graduate school, and these kids have been working constantly at this in the background of their being, "mentally practicing" being married.

### "Tommy Has a Girlfriend!"

"Tommy has a *girlfriend, a girlfriend, a girlfriend,*" mocks his sister Tina.

"I DO NOT! She's just a **friend**," shouts Tommy.

Of course he says that. He's not ready to have a wife and be married! He understands that he is in Marriage Boot Camp, but he's trying to keep it quiet, and *then his "stupid sister" shouts it out.*

Now Tommy is just about ready to start finding out—at least in a very small way—what the consequences of his Family Marriage

Blueprint are. He's having his first meaningful encounter with another human being who has her own Family Marriage Blueprint!

How will that go for him?

Who knows? There are a lot of complicating factors.

He has a Family Marriage Blueprint at this point which includes beliefs on a wide variety of things about relationships: men, women, how you deal with disagreement, what the conversation and affection expectations are, how people get their way and how they react if they don't, and many other aspects of his Blueprint.

They are all there at that first encounter with "HER"

In this first significant encounter, his whole internal world is "on alert."

## If Your Family Marriage Blueprint is mirrored by a person you meet it feels "confirming"

If your Marriage Blueprint calls for you to get along easily, talk easily, smile and have fun, be physical, compliment each other, solve tensions and disagreements with satisfaction and pleasure, and this is exactly what happens, that you do get along easily, talk easily, etc., then you are going to feel "good" and comfortable. You have that "great feeling of all is right in the world."

True also, if your Marriage Blueprint calls for you to squabble, have trouble talking, sneer at each other, be remote, insult each other and have conflict. It is what you expected. Why? Well, it might not be wonderful, but it DOES confirm what you expected, so there's a feeling of things being "correct" or "in balance" in the world, because your expectations are met as predicted.

If you think about your own life, you'll understand that there are things you do that you would "prefer not to do," for example, habits like eating too much, drinking too much, not exercising like you know you should, being undisciplined in your work, etc.

You would "prefer" something different, but when it comes right down to it, you may find that you continue to do the things you don't want to do.

There are two "you's:"

- The "you" that's perfectly happy to continue doing the same things because they are comfortable, familiar, or have some well known effects that this "part of you" is not willing to give up. Sometimes cigarette smokers refer to "the old friend" that's been with them for a very long time, for example.

- And another part of you (an "adopted" part) might think it would be "good for you" to make some changes or develop some new habits or discipline.

Who is it that wins such arguments, as judged by the results? Usually the "old familiar you."

### The Family Blueprint—the Older Blueprint—Is Likely to Win the Battle!

Most of the time, for most of us, the "Family Beliefs" win out, and that's as true in marriage, with the Family Marriage Blueprint, as it is in any other area of life.

Even if we don't really like it (it rains on our picnic), it confirms our expectation and there's something calming and internally harmonious for us. The evidence seeking part of our Belief Systems settles back and says, "I told you so!"

But, what happens if the new girlfriend's Family Marriage Blueprint is very much different from Tommy's?

What if he expects a "mate" who is very quiet, sort of cool physically, reserved about topics such as sex, harmonious and with little disagreement; and the new girlfriend's model calls for noise, disagreement, physical affection or even pushing and shoving, and a little (pre) sexual provocation.

Is it likely that both are going to be a little puzzled by the other's reactions?

I think so.

Thus begins the confusion of living in the adult world where people have different views and habits than yours. How to resolve those differences?

### Marriage "Boot Camp" For Tommy

Tommy comes from a very "demure" and quiet family home. His parents are very polite; the house is quiet and orderly. His parents are very kind, patient and sweet with one another. He's never heard them fight or raise their voices. They are very respectful of one another and rather formal.

This is what he naturally expects to find in intimate relationships, unless he's seen some other powerful models among his family or friends. This is his Blueprint! Thus it will be one thing if he meets a girl he likes who comes from a similar background and acts like it; and another thing if she comes from a dramatically different background, for example, a family where the parents are loud, boisterous, confrontational and unafraid to express their opinions in swear words!

When you hear someone who has a different point of view, do you say, "This person might HAVE something here," or are you more likely to say "this person is crazy and wrong?"

How you frame it is how you see it! If you think difference is good and interesting, you will find difference appealing. If you think difference is threatening and it irritates you, you'll find difference disagreeable— or worse!

### Tommy Meets Kate

Tommy meets Kate and Kate is very quiet and demure around him. He's seen Kate with her friends and she's very boisterous and "out there"—something of the "leader of the pack" with the other girls, and actually gets in some trouble in school.

But around Tommy she's quiet and defers to him.

Tommy likes it and it feels comfortable. He likes this quiet and demure version of Kate and it feels very comforting and interesting to him.

### Tommy Meets Julia
### But What if Her Way of Being with Tommy
### Is The Opposite of His Expectations?

*But then he meets Julia.* Julia is loud, bossy, aggressive, flirtatious, argumentative and very funny!

What's going on here, Tommy might ask.

Maybe he likes it and maybe he doesn't. He's going to have to make a decision. If he likes Julia, he's going to have to consider a new "model" of relationship. Or separate from her. Now that he sees this different way of relating, he has to decide whether to be with Julia and find a way of reconciling the new information, or simply breaking up with her!

### Trying Out a New Model

Tommy decides he likes being around Julia, and tries on a new way of relating, one more like hers. He finds that if he's being more aggressive, louder and more assertive with Julia, she responds positively to it. She seems to really like it when he's like that.

They spend a lot of time together with one another. They go over to each other's houses. Tommy's parents see Julia with him and how she is, and they're not really very happy with it, because to them, Julia seems a little too wild and aggressive. They don't think that Julia is a very good choice in girlfriends for Tommy.

What's happening to Tommy's Marriage Blueprint?

Well, it depends.

He's considering creating a Personal Marriage Blueprint. He's exploring his options. This is a new way of thinking, feeling and believing about relationships.

### Through Julia, He's Seeing the World in A New Way

He now has at least two Marriage Blueprints. He has his Family Marriage Blueprint and a developing Personal Marriage Blueprint.

Why did he start creating the Personal Blueprint? So he could relate to Julia, whom he liked a lot. It's interesting and inviting to him. He enjoys this kind of relating, which seems more fun and a whole new way of viewing and experiencing "being a couple" that he's never seen before. It's a "whole new world," which he enjoys discovering.

But he has his doubts. His parents don't much like Julia, really based on their own Belief System and Marriage Blueprints.

And he feels some internal conflict. His Family Marriage Blueprint (which in this case is shared by his parents) tells him that relationships should be one way, which is harmonious, quiet and calm. And his Personal Marriage Blueprint (which he's developing alongside Julia), gives him the option of being boisterous, loud, argumentative.

### He likes her! He's attracted!
### But what to do about "the family?"
### *The "Romeo and Juliet" Scene*

Sooner or later, Tommy's going to have to face the fact that **being with Julia may be quite uncomfortable.**

The discomfort might very well be worth it if he feels very strongly about Julia! A lot of marriages are established from the beginning with this kind of internal conflict. The only problem is that sooner or later it's likely to be an "issue."

**And the sooner or later comes along very powerfully when and if Tommy and Julia stay together and have children.** Which model to promote to the children? What are we showing them? Are we continuing to be in conflict about what we see as right?

What will Tommy choose to do—and what will Julia choose to do?

Will Tommy continue changing in order to be with Julia?

### Or Will Julia Relent?
### Whose Blueprint Is Going to Dominate?

Will Julia, on the other hand, eventually give up HER model and begin to act more like Tommy's family, with more quiet, more harmony, less arguing, more acquiescence?

In every family, when there are conflicting models, one tends to predominate and be the "primary" way of the family. Usually ONE model wins out and the other one gets defeated—or better said, tends to go "underground." And then it often resurfaces at some later date.

- A large number of people come into marriages with very **different** individual Family Marriage Blueprints from one spouse to the other.
- These differences are often interesting **at the beginning** to both people.
- These differences over time stop being interesting to many couples and start being painful and even competitive or extremely unpleasant.
- There's a tendency for one **Family Marriage Blueprint to "win out" over time.**
- The person whose Family Marriage Blueprint has "lost out" tends to feel like they have given up something very precious

and important to them, and often they feel they should be somehow emotionally or otherwise compensated for their loss.

- The person whose Family Marriage Blueprint "wins out" **feels no obligation** and often doesn't even recognize what the other person has given up to be in marriage with them—because their own Blueprint seems so natural to them.
- This basic conflict can lead to large numbers of **misunderstandings, pain, alienation and even a powerful sense of betrayal.**
- When people feel this conflict between their Family Marriage Blueprint and that of their partner long enough and strongly enough, they eventually have a really powerful feeling and thought **"I'm with the wrong person and this is the wrong marriage for me—I made a terrible mistake."**

For many years they might manage the differences or conflict internally and might not even speak up about it, because they personally have made a "deal" inside of their own heads that in order to be in this marriage, and get the things they like from the marriage, they will put up with or even try to learn to like the fundamental differences between themselves and their partner about what marriage is or should be.

**But let something happen which is seen as a powerful betrayal, and all hell can break loose. All bets are suddenly OFF.**

### Sasha's Silent Deal

Sasha had met Kyle in college. Kyle was kind of wild, a ladies' man, and had a controversial sexual history. He was very social and outgoing, and very popular. A business major who went on to graduate school, he was one of those guys destined for success in the corporate world. His father and mother co-owned a highly profitable business, and they themselves were very socially prominent and involved in the community, and also considered a bit risqué for some of their alleged extramarital affairs.

Sasha is very beautiful and bright, and actually got better grades than Kyle in college. Her professors begged her to continue into graduate school, but she had other ideas. Her dream was to have children and raise a family, and give them a wonderful education and training for the world. She didn't have a great deal of interest in public foundations or high social life like Kyle, and had a strange feeling that this might be a problem.

Kyle agreed with all of her dreams and they had a wild love affair and got married very quickly while still in their junior year together.

They both felt they had made a great marriage, and Kyle confessed even to his best friends that he thought Sasha was the "best thing that ever happened to me." He told Sasha never to worry about the fact that he spent so much time away from home, because he planned to continue to develop his social prominence even if it was without her, as he said, "for the sake of business."

A wonderful compromise which seemed to help everyone.

By the time Kyle was in his third affair (Sasha had conveniently been "unaware" of the other two), she found that this one was too much "in her face" to be ignored, since it was with the mother of one of her children's best friends.

Sasha felt extremely betrayed. She felt she had done her very best to accommodate Kyle in his "ways of being himself," and that she had trusted and believed in him, that she had compromised herself incredibly, and that he was a horrible father, husband and man.

Kyle was at first very remorseful and begged forgiveness. But this turned soon into a kind of sardonic attitude. "After all, Sasha, you knew what I was like and what I wanted in life from the beginning. You would have had to be blind to think otherwise."

### The contracts and agreements you THINK you made

The story of Sasha and Kyle is a dramatic, but not at all uncommon story, of what many couples experience.

There are all kinds of contracts we THINK we are making with our partners, and some of them we make out loud and some of them we "make with our partners inside our own heads," and never tell them about them.

And another kind of contract we make with our partner is with our **fingers crossed** (we don't REALLY intend to keep it).

Maybe you think you know who is to blame for the tremendously painful outcome between Sasha and Kyle.

You do have an opinion about who is responsible and "to blame," don't you?

Maybe you said Sasha, maybe you said Kyle, maybe you said both people; maybe you said neither.

Here's what that judgment says about YOU:

Whichever you said reveals either

- Your Family Marriage Blueprint or
- Your Personal Marriage Blueprint or
- Both.

You might say, "It reveals my religious upbringing," or "It reveals my morals," or even "It reveals my psychological understanding."

But please understand that all of these trainings and sources of your thinking, feeling and believing are the generators of your Belief Systems—and in this situation, your Marriage Blueprint.

So? Well, it matters a great deal how you assign responsibility and value to Sasha and Kyle's responses, to their "hidden contracts," and to their "spoken contracts."

Why?

*Because the way YOU would approach this story* and its ending (or at least temporary ending) helps you understand the thoughts, feelings, beliefs and actions that your Marriage Blueprint would lead you into, and it will also tell you what YOU think is the proper solution.

**But YOUR solution might very well not be your partner's.** And what do you do then? And why is that important?

Remember The Intimacy Paradox? Once again:

---

### Dr. Max's "THE INTIMACY PARADOX"

**The Real Secret of ALL Great Marriages**
**Boils Down To Solving**
**The Intimacy Paradox**

**The Intimacy Paradox is this:**
**100% Acceptance of Yourself**
**PLUS**
**100% Acceptance of Your Spouse**

---

## Just Know What You Are Signing and Why

You might be in one "kind of marriage," and they might be in a very different "kind of marriage." They might have quite different expectations of what marriage is and should be than you. They might believe that men and women should have certain roles or not; they might believe that certain behaviors are OK for them and not for you; they might believe that sex, parenting and money should be handled one way, and you might have a very different set of views.

**You might have certain expectations that your partner never—in all honesty—intends to fulfill.** How would you know? You can only know if you ask, observe, and stay aware.

Only you can decide whether staying in a marriage where you may have compromised your Family Marriage Blueprint continues to be of value to you. You have to assess that regularly.

## Just Knowing This Much Is Power

Fortunately for the first time anywhere, here you'll be able to see clearly those differences outlined. Many people have told me it's a relief just to be able to identify their Marriage Blueprint and that of their partner's, and that it makes things clearer and easier to understand.

*What you see is NOT always what you get.* You might believe that you have an agreement with your spouse on the rules and expectations of each of you in marriage.

However, he or she still might have another Marriage Blueprint working in the background which is far more powerful than anything they might have said to you, even if they felt they were being extremely truthful to you in making those commitments or vows.

## Remember, Beliefs Never Die
## But New Ones—Like a Personal Marriage
## Blueprint—Can Be Born!

The Family Marriage Blueprint that each of us has formed is very strong because it is old and habitual. A new or Personal Marriage Blueprint— if it is far different from the way we were brought up—has to struggle for survival against the power of the older Family Marriage Blueprint.

Since your spouse may have come into the marriage with a different model from yours, you might find this influencing many of your conversations, actions, feelings and reactions. So handling this difference of basic views of marriage can cause a lot of friction, depending on how it is handled!

People who handle these differences smoothly and gracefully tend to have a much better, more enjoyable life. This is what I recommend to you! 100% acceptance of your spouse and his or her Marriage Blueprint!

### "Why Some People Feel Great Almost All the Time And How *You Can Too!*"

Truly understanding that other people are different from you, and being able to accept those differences, is one of the most liberating feelings you will ever have.

As a matter of fact, it is the true requirement for intimacy.

True, some people's inner thoughts and feelings might be similar to yours, but they are never EXACTLY like yours. Truly accepting others makes you an even better, stronger, and deeper person. It feels absolutely wonderful when this happens to you.

It's as if you are given a new body and a new mind, and you are washed clean and given a chance to start over again. The words in religious traditions such as Christianity carry these images: washed by the Blood of the Lamb, Born Again and Saved!

### Sudden Awakening, or Epiphany, Creates a New Sense of Self!

As I said before, it's an exhilarating experience to feel you've finally found something to put your focus in, something which makes sense of your life, and which can guide you and help you in everything you do.

### Belinda and Carl, the Big Change

When Belinda met Carl, she described her life as "OK, in a sort of career girl way." She had a very active life, was working as a tax attorney in Dallas with a big firm, was wealthy and had achieved all her financial goals and career goals by age 38. She had recently been profiled in a national magazine as one of the "top eligible, single women" in her field.

Her parents were very proud of her, and especially her mother, who told her that Belinda had actually "lived the life I would have lived, if I had the courage to do so."

Belinda took this as a compliment, but felt as if she were living someone else's life, not her own; and in fact she was, to a certain extent, living out her mother's dreams.

But Belinda said she didn't know what her own dreams were or had been, and for as long as she could remember, she felt "scripted" to live out the life she was living.

Then she met Carl.

Carl owned a lucrative new car dealership in Dallas. He was the same age as Belinda, and had been married until recently when his wife died tragically young of cancer.

Carl's dream was to have a family and one day close his car dealership and become a full time pastor in his church. He had already spent a month each year serving at a mission in Africa, and his hope and dream was that one day he could provide full time financial, moral and spiritual backing for several missions.

Belinda had come in to the dealership to buy a new car, and Carl was substituting for one of the top salesmen that day, the day that both Carl and Belinda considered "fateful." Belinda's "test drive" or as she later called it, her "testimonial drive" ended up with the two of them having lunch and an invitation for Belinda to come to church with Carl the next Sunday when he was going to give the sermon and lead the congregation.

Belinda felt very squeamish and anxious about going to church, which she had rarely attended in her life, but also had a powerful sense of something important coming her way, both in the man Carl was and in some sense that her life was about to be guided in a brand new way. She felt excited and a little repulsed at the same time, and almost "begged off" on Saturday night when Carl called her to set the time he would pick her up for church the next day.

When she got off the phone, Belinda ran to the bathroom and vomited, thinking this was the weirdest week of her life.

Within six months Belinda had quit her job, was married to Carl, working on becoming pregnant and extremely active in Carl's church, where she said she had "truly found the home I had longed for my whole life."

Of course, Belinda's parents were completely flabbergasted by the whirlwind of events, and felt that somehow their daughter had been inducted into a cult, and that they had lost her. They hoped some day she would "come to her senses," but feared she might be "lost forever"- of course, Belinda felt she had finally been "found."

**How will things go for Belinda from here on?**

**Do you have an opinion or a guess?**

Do you think she will be happy and truly have found her way? Do you think she will get bored being a Fundamentalist Christian wife and churchgoer? Do you think she will take over and be the one to become a qualified pastor before Carl does? Do you believe that the estrangement with her parents will have an influence on what she does from here on? If she has children, how do you think she will parent them? If she has a daughter, what will her message be to the daughter about how to grow up?

**None of us knows yet what will happen, but you have a guess.**

**Your guess is based on your Belief Systems.**

Right?

Whatever filter you see this story through, that filter will determine your interpretation and "guess" about the outcome of this story.

This same filter will determine your judgment of this story, whether you say "hooray for her that she found the Lord," "she's going to wake up from this dream one of these days," "too bad that another brilliant career woman went down the housewife tubes," or any other conclusion you have about the story.

Here's what I say.

**Always be ready to be transformed. Be aware of the power. It can happen to you at any moment and who knows if your life will be better or worse from then on? No one.**

Fortunately, if you don't like it, you can change, come back to your former ways or try something new! It's always up to you!

## Can "Epiphany" Be A Way of Life?

Is it possible for someone to remain in the state of "epiphany," that is, continuously and genuinely open to the new and ready to receive new wisdom and new transformations?

Maybe.

There are certain artists and mystics who seem to claim very sincerely that they are always open and always experiencing epiphany. It might indeed be what the Buddhists call "satori" or the "state of bliss" or certain visionaries experience as the "vision of the All."

You'll see when I describe the "Wild Things" and the "Blissmates" later, that there certainly are many people who live their lives seeking such epiphanies.

**And on the other hand, there might be people who just don't go around judging at all,** or making conclusions much, or reacting to others or the world. They are either incapable of doing so (brain damage) or that's their way of life.

Some Eastern Religions seem to strive for this attitude, and it certainly underlies the philosophy of Zen Buddhism, if not other variations of Buddhism.

For some people, living in a state of perpetual discovery is very exciting and a way of life. For others, it sounds very tiring and not very appealing. Some people would feel dead or empty if they were not continually seeking new pathways into enlightenment, and others would find such a life one of confusion and complete dissatisfaction. It's very important to understand where you stand and your partner stands on the path of spirituality or consciousness, and how you might handle a radical change if it came along.

So in Belinda and Carl's case, what if Carl becomes disillusioned with his faith and decides to stop pursuing these interests? What if Belinda (hard charging person that she is) kind of "overtakes" Carl's leadership in the Church or in the vision-building projects, and Carl doesn't like this or want it anymore, and exhorts and demands Belinda to let him take back the leadership and follow him instead? That would not be terribly unusual for someone of Carl's Marriage Blueprint style. What if Belinda does become bored with this life, and has already had a child?

Life is full of changes. **Your job is to be flexible enough to be prepared for this fact and to move with the changes.**

This is your training.

## 100% Acceptance of Self

What you already are—what you think, believe, feel, how you respond physically, the way you move around in the world, how you respond to criticism and praise, how you handle money, how you feel about intimacy—**everything that you are in this moment is the absolute best and most perfect solution you have come up with about how to be in the world.**

You really don't have to change who you are. But maybe you'd like to. Does this mean you have to become someone else? No. It's not possible anyway. But there are lots of options about how to be in the world, and maybe you'd like to explore them.

### Never Saw His Parents Hug and Kiss

Richard had come to see me as a client when his wife told him that he was "too cold" for her and that he would have to "warm up" if she was going to stay with him. She had sent him into therapy to get fixed, to "get in touch with his feelings."

This demand of his wife's had put Richard into a big internal conflict. He was hurt and a bit confused by his wife's diagnosis of him—and genuinely unsure what it was she was requiring of him. I asked him about his model of a good marriage. He spontaneously began telling me about his experiences as a kid growing up.

Richard told me that he was surprised when he would go over to his friends' houses and see their parents sitting together on the couch talking, sitting with their arms around one another, kissing their children (on the lips!) or giving them long hugs and kisses before they went to school.

He said that he had never actually seen his parents hug and kiss, and that at the age of 8 or 9 years old, his father started shaking his hand rather than hugging him. He said that he kind of liked the feeling that he was "grown up," and shook his father's hand. It felt strong and encouraging, and like he was given a certain respect. But he felt sad and a little lonely about not getting the warmth and affection that other kids got from their parents, and seeing them give that to one another.

He also felt that his parents were very respectful and warm and generous with each other. They were very educated and their conversations about all things under the sun were interesting, and he felt inspired to be smart like them! He liked that each seemed a person in his or her own right.

## Other Parents Seemed Dumb and Shallow

Some of the other parents seemed kind of "dumb and shallow" by contrast, and when he thought about having someone always sitting by you, touching you and putting their arms around you, kissing you all the time and hugging you, it gave him a physical sensation of suffocation.

That's the beginning of an internal dialogue! He now has two different models of how to relate, two different Marriage Blueprints to respond to, and they are inside of him now. It's like an internal debate. He can see, feel, know and believe that there are good qualities to both ways of marriage and family.

Will he be able to combine and integrate those two models? It depends! It depends on all kinds of things: the experiences he has as a young man and his conclusions about them (the data is neutral; but we do interpret it and assign value to it!); the kind of person he meets and her Marriage Blueprints; the religious, philosophical and personal decisions he makes about who he is going to be and how he's going to live; what he concludes is "best for children overall;" and hundreds of other factors.

If he is able to integrate these two models inside of himself and live them in marriage with another person, he might feel an extraordinary sense of achievement and wellbeing. If he finds himself (like most of us) being very strongly drawn to one or another model—either through pressure by his wife and her family or by his own "Personal" model of relationship, or through the loyalty to his family and his family's culture—he'll feel a "split" inside of him.

In the case of this split, one of the "good things" has to be chosen over another, or better said, it will "be chosen" because most of us never even think about the view that we are choosing, what we believe and how we act on it. We just live life and try to figure out what happened later!

So Richard is caught in this feeling of ambivalence. Something will feel "missing" in his life if he lives more by one Marriage Blueprint than by another. Something inside of him (an "Opposing" Belief System) will just continue working on "getting its way."

For example, if he would have had the kind of marriage his parents had—which was respectful but a bit cool and distant and detached—something inside of him will be always looking for that "other" kind of life, the one with lots of hugs, kisses, warmth and affection. The likelihood that he will have an affair, either emotionally, or physically and sexually, with an attractive woman who comes along and shows great interest in him, is very strong.

But he now had a wife who had grown up in one of those warm, affectionate and expressive families. Her model of a good marriage and a good family life called for far more physical and emotional expression than Richard was used to. She assured him that she did respect him and was proud of his intelligence and his skills, but she also wanted more warmth and affection and feelings.

What I was able to show him was that he could actually live in "both worlds." He could keep his sense of reserve and properness. He could expect his wife to respect him and he respect her. They could have great conversations and keep intellectually stimulated and alive.

And still at the same time he could reap the benefits of a marriage relationship with lots of affection, warmth, great sex and enjoyment. The "worlds" or Marriage Blueprints were not in any kind of mutual exclusion! They could both exist and together combine the best of both worlds.

Richard was afraid that he would lose some of himself if he were too emotionally or physically expressive. He feared losing the qualities of what he admired in his own parents. But yet he also longed for more closeness with his wife and more enjoyment with her. When he realized that he could "have his cake and eat it too," he was quite delighted and within a few sessions and conversations with his wife, Richard was really enjoying his marriage—and his wife was too!

He solved the Intimacy Paradox! He found in his own life the answer to that magic code: 100% acceptance of yourself, and 100% acceptance of your spouse!

It was up to Richard to decide whether it was worth it to him to make those shifts in his internal beliefs and actions to have happiness and satisfaction in his marriage. It was worth it to him, because he already had fascination with and appreciation of a different "model of being" in marriage. His desire was strong and his willingness to be open to change was great. Plus he had good guidance from me. It's a good combination.

### Maybe You'd Like Some New Options If Your Old Ones Aren't Going So Well

You can choose the marriage you want! Whatever conflicts you may be having in your marriage are going to be settled either by solving The Intimacy Paradox and becoming truly married, or headed to divorce. Either option is fine. Any option is fine. More than likely what is already available in your marriage, if you managed it differently inside your own head and heart, would go a long way toward creating a great marriage. But you can choose.

Choose what you want, like at a buffet.

Wouldn't that be nice? *Already* you might find that a lot of things are changing in you that are kind of unexpected, and that you are discovering things about yourself, about beliefs and about marriage that were unknown to you, but which are potentially very satisfying and fulfilling.

*And isn't it nice to know that there really isn't anything wrong with you at all?* And that you get to use your wisdom and knowledge and skills that you already have to mold and build a new and wonderful life for yourself. And that it isn't even that hard to do, and that it has already started happening in you.

*And isn't it nice to know that there really isn't anything wrong with others at all?* And that they also have the choice to use their wisdom and knowledge and skills that they already have to mold and build a new and wonderful life for themselves. And that it isn't even that hard to do, and that they might possibly at any moment choose to do so and potentially change very rapidly, but they also might not, and that even if they don't there is nothing at all wrong with that either?

*And isn't it nice to know that all the information and data coming at you in this wild world is just neutral* after all, until you assign it a meaning? And that you personally, you yourself get to assign the meaning to it you wish to, and like to. And that nobody can stop you from doing this. And that you are free as a bird to see whatever goes on in this world as you like, only by understanding and recognizing the Belief System that you have, knowing its power and learning how to either live by this Belief System or how to go ahead and make a brand new Belief System, and learn how to funnel energy into it?

Maybe you think this book will be the ***best thing that ever happened to you!***

# CHAPTER SIXTEEN

## Control your Destiny Throwing a Simple Mental Switch

Now you understand that you are driven by your beliefs. You know where they came from, how you created them, and how they influence everything you do.

You know you have a choice whether to follow the "given" beliefs or to create some new ones and follow those.

Wouldn't it be great to know how to simply make changes with this knowledge?

Think of a Belief System as a reservoir of energy, or a "jar" full of energy. This "jar" contains the thoughts, feelings, body memory and history of "evidence-scanned" through your life in it, all that it is allowed to gather.

**Imagine a big funnel on top of each Belief Jar,**
**Like a piggy bank, waiting to be filled.**

The Jar is a reservoir of energy waiting to be used by you! Think of a gas tank full of fuel or a battery that has gotten charged and is ready to run what you hook up to it.

All kinds of data comes along every single day: words, gestures, physical actions, and behaviors by other people; reactions to you and your words, movies, radio, television, music; advertisements in every imaginable form; weather; your environment, including where you live, your house or apartment or the place in the world you live; thousands of other pieces of information and other data, or even millions, every day.

It's coming, coming, coming at you. What will you do with it?

What you pay attention to are the things that support your beliefs.

If you believe that people are kind and thoughtful and generous, you'll particularly notice kindness, thoughtfulness and generosity.

If you believe that people are selfish, thoughtless, greedy and self-serving, you'll particularly notice selfishness, greed and egotism.

**All this information is thrown into the funnel, and into the Jar it goes.**

Further evidence of the belief.

Evidence in support of your "case!"

## These Laws are our Belief Systems

So all of this data goes into the funnel, and into the Jar, and once in the jar, it is treated as clear evidence of "The Truth" by you.

Your Jar gets full, and you point to how full the Jar is to demonstrate the "fullness" of your Truth. Look at all the evidence gathered! Beyond a shadow of a doubt! A preponderance of evidence for my Truth! See how full that Jar is!

Maybe you take the top off of the Family Beliefs Jar and move a ton of the data over to your Personal Beliefs Jar. Then that one is the new "Truth."

That's going to change things!

Early on, you didn't have much choice. When you were an impressionable child, your belief system Jars just got filled "for you." But now, you get to decide!

Will it be your Family Beliefs Jar, or Personal Beliefs Jar? Will it be your Family Marriage Blueprint that is supported, filled, given more energy, more "proof"—or a newer, Personal Marriage Blueprint?

## A Simple Model of Total Life Change

You just start filling that new Jar. All the data and information that comes to you in your life, you start pitching into that funnel that will fill the new Jar.

If you'll remember back to James, the man who wanted to become "undepressed" who we spoke of earlier, he had a "Depression-Generating Belief System," or let's call it now: a "Depression-Generating Jar."

All he could see was evidence of how awful his life and the world were. That's because he threw everything that came at him into that Depression Jar.

The Jar got full, and he said, "See, I'm right. Life is depressing."

Remember, I gave him an experiment to do. I said, "Try to look for evidence for the opposite of things you see now, and let's see if you gather that evidence."

It was an experiment, but I cheated. I knew he was very much ready to start a new Jar.

His Depression-Generating Jar was just not functional or interesting or rewarding enough for him anymore! He decided that it was truly time for a change, and said he would "do anything to become undepressed."

So, I just fashioned a new Jar for him. This one we could call the "I'm Resourceful and Find the World and People in it a Good Place Belief System" Jar; or, more simply, "The World is Good" Jar.

Once he started using this filter, and pitching data and information into the "World is Good" Jar, he got "undepressed" very rapidly.

Remember, it took him only a week! And remember I showed you how rapidly very powerful and dramatic change can happen.

But also remember I said that it requires intense desire, focus and determination, along with knowledge of how it's done.

Well, in case you are interested, this is exactly how it's done. I'll review quickly for you here so you can immediately start using the method if you like.

This works powerfully on any kind of belief you are trying to change, and even (if very conscientiously applied) on very long-standing addictions. You have to be the one to supply the "content" (what you want to change) and I'll supply the "how"—here I'm using the example of James and his depression (he wanted to change to an "undepressed" way of life).

Want to try it? Here's how.

Take out a piece of paper.

What would you like to change? Your views about money? About other people? About yourself? About your marriage? About your children? About your job, your vocation?

I recommend you write about marriage.

On the left, write all the currently held beliefs, thoughts and feelings about the topic. It could be about marriage and what it means to you; it could be about your religious beliefs; it could be about your relationship with money; it could be about your current parenting.

**Left Column:**      **Right Column:**
**"Current Beliefs"**      **"New Beliefs I'm Creating"**

Your experiment has 2 requirements:

- Very strong desire to change a basic belief, because the one you are using truly doesn't work for you, and
- An open and honest and genuine willingness to write out your current Belief System and how it affects you. And a willingness to take several hours out of your life to do this.

So in James's story, he really wanted to stop being depressed and live life on better terms. He was losing faith in life, losing confidence in himself, and his family was getting sick and tired of him.

He had a set of beliefs that were working overtime inside of him. So on the **left** column, he wrote his set of beliefs that include:

- I'm at the age where death comes soon to men in my family.
- Because I'll die soon, nothing has much meaning.
- Other people are lazy and looking for a way out.
- There's really not much more in the world than bad news.
- All I do in life is struggle against the odds and try to be happy.
- People are always demanding things of me and are never satisfied.
- I'll never be happy or joyous and what's the use anyway if I'm going to die soon.

You might need help from a friend, your spouse or a therapist to actually come up with these kinds of statements.

So now, on the **right** column of your piece of paper, I want you to write the new or "Personal" Belief System that you are ready to test.

In James's case, here's the **new Belief System** he signed on for, to "scan for evidence" for and to "prove" inside of himself (this would be his "right column"):

- I am possibly an anomaly to the idea that men of my age die young, and possibly a new and interesting version of men in my family.

- Even if I died tomorrow, I want to be able to take my last breath saying "Wasn't yesterday interesting as can be?"
- There's a ton of extremely interesting and varied people in the world, I can't wait to talk to and understand all their different ways of living and thinking and feeling; to that end, I'm going to start conversations with everyone I can by asking them an interesting question.
- There's definitely a lot of news going on in the world, but perhaps it's the harbinger of fascinating new developments that will bring unprecedented spiritual development in the world; you can't make omelets without breaking eggs. I wonder what the new omelet will be?
- Every day I have the resources to find some new way to make my life easier and more effective.
- People love me so much and respect me so much they can't wait to get my help and involvement in their lives. That's why my wife so frequently has new projects for me to do.
- Even if I die tomorrow, today I'm going to have as much fun as possible.

**This is a model of kind of "Personal Belief System" you write on the right side of your paper! It's a "new" way of seeing the same information! Remember, data is neutral until we do something with it!**

Write out the "right column." Then you just go around your world looking for evidence of this new Belief System! Every piece of information or data that comes along you just "toss into the funnel" of your new Belief System.

Because you are deliberately changing your thinking and the filter through which they "process data" from your world, your nimble and powerful mind will be looking very actively for evidence of this new Personal Belief System.

The mind is incredible.

### The mind will actually do anything we instruct it to do

If we tell it to look for pain, struggle and misery and never figure out a way to solve it; it will do that flawlessly for us. If we tell it to look for joy, simple solutions and pleasure, and a way to solve things we experience in life; it will do THAT flawlessly for us!

But you have to give it instructions.

This is a method of giving your mind instructions on what to look for and then what to do with what you find—how to filter and then how to sort the information that comes your way!

You must start with giving your mind instructions if you are going to create new and different results in your life.

You must NOT be guided by your feelings first and foremost, because your feelings are determined by your old Family Belief System and will keep you in a rut, doing the same thing over and over again.

**Your mind will follow instructions**

**Your thinking will progress along a new pathway→**

**Then your feelings will follow→**

**And the new Belief System will become a habit and a way of life**

You'll perhaps feel a little excitement, perhaps anxiety, then some discomfort or a little frustration, then pleasure, followed by happiness, relief and a sense of wellbeing and accomplishment.

Then these emotions or feelings will be followed by the experience of "Aha! I see how this is done!" And the recognition that pretty much anything in your life can be re-directed by this methodology.

**So now you will have a new Belief System**

And you get to decide how full you want to make it, how prominent, how powerful.

This is up to you.

Ok, let's lay out the choices of belief systems or "blueprints" for marriage.

# PART THREE

**Your Marriage Blueprint™**
*Belief Systems in Action*
The Models upon Which Your Marriage Is Built
And How Choosing the One You Love
Can Radically and Positively Transform Your Marriage

# CHAPTER SEVENTEEN

## The Four Compass Points in Marriage:
### Uniqueness v. Tradition, North/South

### (Four Cardinal Directions:
### Uniqueness versus Tradition
### Pleasure versus Duty)

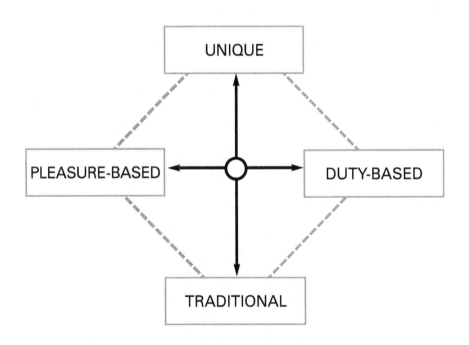

**Marriage Blueprint Map**

Your Marriage Blueprint map is like a compass. It has a North, a South, an East and a West.

**Overlaid on this are two styles: Independence and Joining.** Altogether this produces 8 basic Marriage Blueprints.

I'll tell you about each Pole (north–south, east–west), and then the two Styles, and then I'll show you the 8 Marriage Blueprints!

Please remember the following points:

- **There are no "normal" or "abnormal" directions or Styles,** they all are naturally occurring and there are plenty of people who are strong examples of any of them.
- When you have identified your basic Direction and Style, and your spouse's basic Direction and Style, this is the **first step in the conversation, not the last one.**

### It's All about Tendencies and Preferences, Not Absolutes

Let me give an analogy with directions.

### Example of "Tendencies"—Heading West

You might be on State Highway 44 West, headed generally west. However, the highway might at times be headed northwest, southwest, or at times in a dogleg in the road, it might even be headed straight north or straight south. And while you are driving along it might get to be late at night, and you are sleepy. Say you've passed through a town ten miles back and suddenly realize there's not another town with motels for fifty more miles. You turn around and go back to the town, so you can get some sleep. Does this mean you stopped your journey west?

### You were going west, you still are

No, it just means you went back the other direction because you wanted to, for a reason that made sense to you.

You might be on State Highway 33, headed north. Along the way you decide to go camping at a lake that is east of the highway, and the highway actually angles back south for a while. Does this mean you aren't generally headed north? Not at all. It just means you took a detour.

So when I talk about the Four Directions and the Two Styles, please understand that I am talking about "basic Directions," and not about some absolute, set in stone, unchangeable fact about you, or something that you couldn't change if you wanted to. You can always choose a new direction.

You have a Family Belief System, which you accompany with thoughts, feelings, a body which has its own needs, desires, health or disease, your looks and appeal, your experience, your education, and all the other things that go together to make the person you know as yourself.

Even though there's no one else exactly like you, there are plenty of people who share similar Belief Systems to yours. Otherwise, the influences of all those people and circumstances could never have had any effect on you at all. When your Belief System evolves and grows, you will always have a sense of identity to a set of natural tendencies and people, even if perhaps that group of people and tendencies might be extremely small.

What I'd like you to do during this part of the book is look at these descriptions and see what you think applies to

- You
- Your spouse.

## "Uniqueness-Orientation"

In the "Uniqueness-Orientation" to marriage, the following things are prized **very highly** in marriage:

- Discovery and Experimentation

If you have a strong "Uniqueness-Orientation" as part of your Marriage Blueprint, you have a strong belief that marriage should be a continuous and very powerful *path of discovery.* You might very well think of marriage as "The Path," or the most important route to personal discovery that there is.

Discovery and experimentation—not so much the results of that discovery and experimentation—are the point!

### Newness, you love what is new

If you have a "Uniqueness-Orientation," *you are always interested in what can be "new" in your marriage.*

You might get very bored with what other people would consider a wonderfully settled and calm life.

**You like change,** and even evaluate the importance of whatever you do in life by the measurement of whether it produces change or not, and offers new and exciting "difference" in your marriage.

### Evolution of the marriage to greater realms

You want your marriage to **truly grow!** You are not satisfied with the "usual realms" of life together. You are perhaps interested in deep spiritual traditions such as Tantra, Eastern and Western spiritual practices, or you are driven to go to workshops.

You might buy lots of books, seminars, or videos to continue your study of relationships. You want to pursue the elusive goal of intimacy! It's vitally important to you, and you may always be in pursuit of this moving target!

You are very willing to "try new experiences" in life, even if they seem kind of "far out" to most people.

### Distinction from "The Crowd"

Your marriage needs to be "unique" and leave its own mark. You might be a model to others in your circle or in the seminars and studies you do. *You see something special about your relationship or marriage that others might benefit from learning!*

And yet, you have some sense that you understand and possess some special wisdom that most people will probably never grasp, even though they should!

You know you are a little "different from others"—those others who are quite happy to, in your words "live in front of the TV" or whatever else it is they do.

You have your own ways of living that you have considered and done because you know they will provoke you to newness.

Sometimes it's a little lonely, being a pioneer, but it's worth it to you. You are a little "misunderstood" by some of your friends because they think you are just trying to be special or different to get noticed, but you know it's because of a value of yours, not because of some "ego" thing.

Uniqueness is hard to define, but it is clearly something powerful which excites the imagination. Uniqueness is, well, unique!

You would be happy if someone looked at your marriage and family and said, "Wow, they are certainly doing things their own way. It looks like it's always something new around there!"

---

## "Uniqueness" Opinions and Views about:
### Sex

You think people are too hung up on sex—and this is because they are stuck in "standard" definitions of what sex is. If they would loosen up a little and go more deeply into what sex really is, they would feel a lot better about sex.

Your Marriage Blueprint leads you to see sex as *one* of the most powerful pathways to discovery in marriage!

You understand people who are experimental with sex, and people who have different orientations than you. Your view of sex in marriage might be a bit shocking to others. Your own practices might not be very controversial or experimental (though they probably are in some ways), but your ideas of what is possible, interesting and accepted are much wider and more tolerant than most people's.

**If you are a member of a "traditional" religious organization, you are always bringing in a new element into it, such as a more progressive discussion about sex.** You believe extremely strongly in tolerance and acceptance and even encouragement of difference!

Your view of your own sexuality may be open to discovery. It wouldn't surprise you at all if you had sexual orientations or interests that you've never explored or known about before.

You may even like the idea (even if you wouldn't try it) of experimenting with sex toys or alternative methods of stimulation, possibly group sex or sex with other partners even within a committed relationship such as marriage!

You look at sex as a wonderful mystery and a method of self and partner discovery. Even though you aren't against sex for procreation —just the opposite perhaps because the experience of pregnancy and the changes it brings fascinate you—your view of sex is far wider than this, and you think of sex as "just one of the parts of a life of discovery and deepening understanding, love, acceptance and tolerance."

---

You like sex, and wish everyone did. But you perhaps don't like it as others do. Others might focus on orgasms, or how it's such an essential part of a standard marriage. Others might focus on the notion of the "marital duty" that is included in marriage.

You don't see sex as a duty—you are more likely to think of it as a "role-play" than take it deadly seriously.

## Parenting and Kids

You see children as a source of true wonder and potential, a miracle on the planet.

In your Marriage Blueprint, children are miracles of discovery and can add through their unique vision and wisdom that they bring to the family—and their own personal development helps us all grow.

You love seeing their discoveries most of all—and are far less interested in whether they learn the "standard" rules of their society, or the "standard" subjects of school taught in the "standard" schools. You think children should have every opportunity to discover their own uniqueness and not be "pressed in a mold" by any organization, church or school district rules.

Others might SAY they believe in the importance of individuality and individual expression of children as they grow up, but it is a SACRED thing to you!

You might home-school your children, or you might have them in public school so they can see what "ordinary kids" do so they can have those experiences.

If your child is athletic, you don't see any reason why he or she shouldn't also be interested in poetry or dance. You encourage variety and, uniqueness! You see everything as "experience" and "learning" for kids and don't think that kids should be "kept in a box" in any way, but given chances to express their specialness.

Your motto is "experiences," "opportunities" and not "memorizing data" unless that's something that will increase experiences or allow your child to experience the world in a new way.

You want your children to be exposed to as much "difference" as they can be in this world, and don't like the idea of limiting children in any way.

## Money

Money serves the purpose of giving opportunity for experiences.

In your Marriage Blueprint, money serves to make marriage richer and deeper, by giving you an opportunity to explore and discover and "make it new!"

Money gives you opportunity for discovery and learning about yourself and your partner. Money can certainly be used to buy things, but those things aren't for the purpose of security or "having" or acquiring.

Money is for being and doing! Money lets you do what you want to do in the world to increase your discovery and knowledge.

Money lets you do what you need to do to promote discovery, and experiment with life. Whether education, travel, therapy, going to cultural experiences, music, sports events—whatever increases your experiences of the world—that's what money is for.

## Personal Development

One of the most important things in life is personal development. The universe is infinite and your interest in it can never end. You want to "be there" in the middle of change and development, and if you miss something that's important to you, it's like you have lost something of deep value.

Marriage is about personal development for you, you consider it a natural and important part of personal development, and maybe one of the biggest sources of mystery and meaning that exists.

## Religion and Spirituality

You probably have a powerful spiritual center in your Belief System, although you may or may not go to church or any kind of "formal" arrangement of religion. You might still define yourself as a follower of a certain religious tradition, but you are going to practice it "in your own way."

Your Marriage Blueprint calls for uniqueness in how you practice your religion or spirituality.

Even if you do attend formal religious practices, you have found your own special way of doing so. You might belong to a special splinter group or a group that studies the Holy Books on a whole other path than the "ordinary congregation."

It's not that you are "against" religious practices, but you may see religion as even a "roadblock" to spirituality.

You might rather join a group of others who meet on the beach and see God through the sun over the ocean, or in a trip to see the fly outs of the eagles from their rookeries at dawn; you can see the unique and special version of religion or spirituality through your own approach.

You might even claim that the way you practice religion or spirituality is "even more traditional than those who call themselves traditional," because your methods are older and more like those of the early devotees of your religion.

In this as in every other area of your life together.

## "Tradition-Orientation"

In contrast to the "Uniqueness-Orientation," if your preference is for "Tradition-Orientation" you are focused on deepening the time-honored and time-tested wisdom of the ages, of the elders and of the prophets, saints, Buddhas or other guides and patriarchs of your tradition.

One thing must not be confused. Creativity and invention is not the sole province of the Uniqueness Blueprint—if you are Tradition-Oriented, you can also find individual and highly creative expression, but the difference is that it will always be within the guidance of your tradition.

If your Marriage Blueprint is driven by a "Tradition-Orientation," these are among the things you prize very highly:

- You are part of an identified tradition that you honor and respect very highly.
- You cherish the feeling of belonging to something so deep and meaningful with a powerful history that is at the root of your Belief System.
- It is clear to you that there are right ways and wrong ways to live, and your tradition specifies those ways—they were put here for us to follow.

- The guidance of tradition may develop over the years to a certain degree, but it is based on historical foundations which are much bigger than the individual and the individual's ability to define them.
- Your belief is that whatever is wrong in the world is because of deviation from the tradition which, you believe, offers the best answers to life's questions.

**You are a person whose respect for the traditions you follow is central to your life.** You may sometimes feel that you are imperfect or even quite wayward in your following of that tradition, but to you the tradition is what "should" be followed.

*Your Marriage Blueprint is directly tied to the tradition you follow.*

Now, of course, that tradition might be a Family Belief System (the one you grew into as a child), or it might be one you chose later (Personal Belief System). It might, of course, be in conflict with another, perhaps a Uniqueness-Orientation driven Belief System inside of you.

But you have chosen Tradition.

By all that you now hold sacred and meaningful, you are a Tradition-Oriented person, and your Marriage Blueprint (whether Personal or Family) reflects that in your thoughts, feelings and actions. Everything is intended to be in complete agreement with your tradition.

You are throwing all the data that comes your way into the funnel of the Jar of "Tradition"—doing your best to follow the best practices and teachings of your tradition.

Whatever it is that you say about your Tradition-Orientation, it's clear that the focus on tradition is a focus on your relationship to, and evaluation by, your traditional doctrines and guidelines.

What is the tradition that you follow? If you can answer the question, it might be a good sign that you are Tradition-Oriented; many people wouldn't even understand the question. If you do, then you probably have focused on and thought about your tradition for a long time.

One thing to make very clear. You don't have to be ORTHODOX in your tradition to be Tradition-Oriented. If you are an innovator within your tradition, but are still essentially guided by it, then you are still Tradition-Oriented.

And if you are "in-synch" with your tradition, it's going to create a feeling of well-being in you.

**You would be happy if someone looked at your marriage and family and said, "Now There's a Strong Traditional Marriage."**

Even if your own actual definition of "tradition" is quite different from theirs!

## Sex

**The definition, place, and meaning of sex in marriage are defined by your tradition.** If you are very close to the tradition you follow, you already know your guidelines and how you should be thinking, feeling and believing about sex.

Although some of the teachings might be uncomfortable or you might have some disagreement with those teachings, you still know what the "correct" way to think and feel about those things would be, and you know that what is needed is for you to find peace and acceptance of the teachings.

In some traditions, sex is *primarily* or even *only* for the purpose of procreation and giving birth to children who are brought into the world to continue the tradition. That may or may not be the teachings of your tradition. But whatever your tradition, since it is a tradition with depth and history, you know the place of sex in it and where you ought to be in your views of it.

And as such, you might (if you are religious) view sex as a *sacrament and gift to humans from their Creator.* It's a sacred act and should never be defiled or practiced only for selfish interests.

In other traditions, you view sex in marriage with a special eye, as something that can be enjoyed freely under the guidance of that tradition, and is viewed as a source for ultimate connection (within the tradition), and creates a sense of belonging to the tradition and to one another.

In your "Tradition-Oriented" Marriage Blueprint, the definitions of what is acceptable sexually are presented as inviolable and defined. You know what the right way is to practice sex.

## Parenting and Kids

In your "Tradition-Oriented" Marriage Blueprint, your guidance about how to raise your children is clear, and handed down from your tradition.

Again, that tradition might be one of the "Big Religions" on earth, or it might be something less well known, such as Rudolph Steiner's Anthroposophy, the origins of the Waldorf Schooling System; or even more local and less known than that. But it is a tradition and you are dedicated to its precepts.

Your job is to bring up children to be faithful and loyal followers of the tradition. As a modern parent (but with Traditional Orientation), your job is to find the approaches using what has been studied about how people learn best, and to use this information to best bring your children into the fold of the tradition.

Even if you have not been a particularly fervent disciple of your tradition, you do know what the teachings are, and now that you have children of your own, you feel some draw toward "letting them have a chance" to be part of the tradition.

If you are a strong disciple of your tradition, you will find a way to think about your children and their potential resistance to the teachings; you know that children can be unruly and questioning, and will find a way to guide them with a steady hand into the tradition that is so important and central to your Marriage Blueprint.

Your children are an extension of you, according to your tradition, and are the ones who will be around to carry on the tradition when you no longer are able to do so. So they must be taught well.

### Money

Your Marriage Blueprint calls for a judicious and deliberate use of money for the glory of your tradition and its service. You may well be taught to give a percentage, such as a tithe (tenth) of your income, to the continuation of your tradition.

You may believe that money is the gift of the Divine to us to preserve our families and our relationships. In any case, money serves the purpose of giving you the chance to properly serve your tradition.

It is for our security and wellbeing and for the protection and nurture of your family and marriage. It's to be used wisely and partly as a hedge against the impact of the world around you, not to invite every single influence of the world around you.

Money is made from the exercise of your special gifts and talents given to you by the Divine, and is to be used to praise and honor your tradition.

Your Marriage Blueprint leads you to see money as a commodity of value to be used to help you and your family preserve and advance your tradition.

### Personal Development

In Your Marriage Blueprint, your personal development is directed toward your deepening and growth in your tradition.

If it is a *religious* tradition, personal development is finding the way that the Divine can shine through you into the world more fully. You are the servant of the Divine, and your marriage is in the service of this Divine source and its honor and glory.

**You are the vessel through which your tradition shines.**

What is personal is to be subsumed under the power and glory of your tradition.

When you have problems, it is because you are somehow out of line with your tradition.

When your marriage is out of line or full of conflict that harms you or your children, it is because you are out of line with your tradition, and the answer lies in you returning to the source and guidance of your tradition.

All of the answers are within the tradition, and if you go deeply enough you will find all the answers you seek. "Seek and ye shall find," but there are good ways and bad ways to seek. These ways are stated or implied in the teachings of your tradition.

### Religion and Spirituality

In your Marriage Blueprint, the Tradition Oriented Belief System guides you to the proper place that marriage is to serve in your life.

Religion is usually the cornerstone of the Tradition-Orientation (though not always), but whatever that cornerstone is for you, it most definitely has guidance for you about how you should practice your spirituality.

There is guidance that you are to follow in how to worship, and your marriage is to be part of that worship.

# CHAPTER EIGHTEEN

## Fun or Work First?
### Pleasure-Orientation V. Duty-Orientation
### East/West

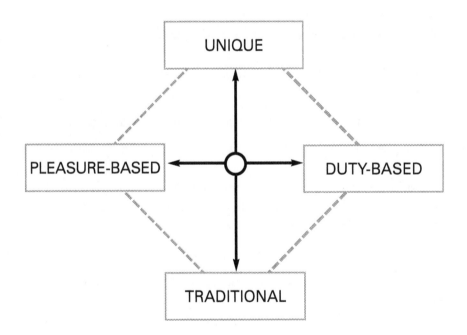

**Marriage Blueprint Map**

If Uniqueness and Tradition are the North and South of your Marriage Blueprint Directions, Pleasure-Based and Duty-Based Orientations are the *other* axis of your Belief System.

# The Pleasure-Based Orientation

If your Marriage Blueprint is driven by the *Pleasure-Based* Orientation, you are called to seek pleasure in your married life as a primary way of living in marriage.

First, I want to make it clear that just because you are Pleasure-Based doesn't mean to imply that you are not responsible! You may very well be the most responsible people we could ever meet!

But it's not your first choice of WHY to do something—to fulfill a duty! You might have found a way to fulfill duties very efficiently, but it's not what you prefer at all.

You prize these things very highly:

- Enjoyment of all the good things life offers
- Play! You might be a hard worker also, but what you dream about and what drives you is **play**
- The experience more than the "product" of your efforts, and
- You celebrate life!

### Enjoyment of all the good things life offers

Marriage is a great opportunity (or should be) to enjoy life together with a partner, in your view!

Marriage allows even more chance to enjoy life than you could get on your own. Life is all about wonderful experiences, and how great is it that you get to experience these with a partner in life?

### Play, It's the point!

As I said, you might work hard, but the real, true point of living is to be able to *play hard.*

Whatever your passions are, the *point of being married* is to be able to share those passions, and have support and encouragement through marriage in those passions, together or apart.

### It's the experience, not the product
### The Pleasure-Orientation: *Celebrate* Life!

You are far less concerned about whether you have a "perfect" marriage, or meet up to someone or some organization's standards or definitions of what marriage and family should be about, than you are about whether you are enjoying your life together.

*To you it really is about "stop and smell the roses" in your life together.* Celebration of your marriage and life together is absolutely as important, if not MORE important, than what you are actually doing.

You enjoy marking events together, having gifts and surprises, you like to emphasize and celebrate all accomplishments or anniversaries. It's not because you have to, it's because you WANT to.

You get a lot out of marking events in your life together. You keep a lot of photographs, mementos, souvenirs and cherish them in the way that they bring back pleasure.

It's not nearly so much pride of accomplishment as it is in *enjoyment of the moment.*

Your motto in life is a special twist on "It's not whether you win or lose, but how you play the game."

**Your motto is "are we having fun yet?"—because what's the point of doing anything if it's not fun?**

This view of life—as being right when it is fun—drives your Marriage Blueprint. You are up when there's enjoyment and down when there is drudgery and nothing but duty.

*A Great Marriage to you is one in which love and enjoyment are both present as much as possible.* The reason that you do the duties in life is so that you can afford the lifestyle and pleasures you so greatly enjoy.

In a 24 hour day, if you had your choice, fun and enjoyment would take up as much of the 24 hours as is possible, how about all of it?

### *"Play first, work later!"*

Because you have a Pleasure-Orientation, you prefer, instead of the motto "Work first, play later," "Play first, work later!" A friend of mine, Carla, has a motto when she goes out to eat in restaurants, "Eat dessert first, you never know!"

In other words, emphasis on what a person becomes versus what he or she does, is more important to you. Life is not "tasks" to you, or "mere duty," but a wonderful experience to be received.

Marriage, to you, is about pleasure. How easy it is for others to misunderstand you and judge you—those who are driven by duty, and are so righteous in their position about pleasure.

Fortunately, you can directly experience pleasure and know it needs no explanation or rationalization.

**You would be happy if others looked at your marriage and your family and said, "They look like they really are enjoying life."**

Let's look at how you view some of the parts of your marriage and married life together.

## Sex

Well, sex certainly isn't some kind of "chore" or duty to you!

Good sex is fun sex!

You feel that sex is one of those "ties that bind," and really one of the most important ones.

You view sex as just part of the picture of enjoyment of life. It's no huge deal in itself, because it's just one of the over-all parts of a marriage, defined by the pleasure it brings to people in the marriage.

If people would just relax a little, they would be able to enjoy sex more and not be so worried or concerned about it, don't you agree?

## Parenting and Kids

Children are a *joy* to you—they should be, or else you probably shouldn't even have any!

If you do have children, one of your views about kids is that these days, kids are forced to grow up too fast! Let the kids be kids! Right? They should be allowed to be kids as long as possible, and not pushed into adulthood.

Your view of discipline is to help and encourage them to get their work (such as schoolwork) done as soon as possible, so they can get around to the most important part of life, which is enjoying yourself!

Your questions to kids is not "are you staying out of trouble," but "are you having fun yet?" You might be a bit of a "big kid" yourself, and kind of wish you could live your childhood again—and have even more fun this time around.

Again, if you have children, one of the things you most look forward to are things you can do together to enjoy. Things everyone loves. Your idea of a perfect outing with the kids is one in which everyone has a good time, and remembers that good time when you are talking about it later.

If you don't have children, it might be because you feel very honestly that the enjoyment you are having in life and plan to keep having, well, you don't want it to end by your being confined by children, and the duties and responsibilities they bring.

## Money

What is the purpose of having money? Your Marriage Blueprint is clear about this: to have fun and enjoy life!

You like having and spending. Depending on your Style of Marriage Blueprint (we'll discuss in the next section), it's either on your own independent interests, or on your mutual interests, but it's all about the spending, either way.

If you are an outdoors enthusiast, the "Sportsmen Shows" in the exhibition halls love to see you coming! You are going to see plenty of stuff you like.

If you are a book collector, someone is looking for that special first edition for you.

If you are an artist, your basement is full of art you've done, that maybe one day you'll get around to selling.

If you love music, you can't wait until the next concert of your favorite musical group, even though the tickets are kind of outrageous.

If you have a hobby of any kind that involves equipment (fishing rods, sewing machines, car-racing, and crafts, for example), you know that "good equipment is FAR much better than mediocre or poor stuff." You have the best!

And if you don't get much pleasure out of stuff, but out of things like travel and events (such as concerts, art exhibits, hanging out all over the world), your "collection" will be of experiences.

## Personal Development

Your Marriage Blueprint gives plenty of latitude in the areas of personal development, but the main word is "passion."

You like encouraging personal development in your marriage as long as it is in the pursuit of a passionate and enjoyable experience!

Again, the Pleasure-Based Orientation drives this part of your Belief System.

If something is going to be pursued, by all means, let's pursue it, as long as it gives you something you like and desire.

### Religion and Spirituality

If you find a church, temple or mosque where they understand that religion and spirituality must touch the heart, soul and body, you are there!

You are not going to follow a religious teaching just because it tells you what to do and how to do it. You are quite happy to follow rules or guidelines if they really do create a sense of wellbeing and joy in you, but the minute it becomes drudgery or a "downer," you are not interested anymore.

Religion presented through its music and art, now that stands a chance with you, because it appeals to your sense of beauty, enjoyment and inspiration.

Religion's purpose is to inspire you to experience!

If it helps you experience directly the beauty, wonder and mystery of the Divine Creation, you are going to be interested. If it's all about lecturing and moralizing and telling you what you should be doing, you are most definitely not going to be interested!

# The Duty-Based Orientation

Now we go over the other "pole" of "East and West," which is the "Duty-Based Orientation."

Let me remind you that these categories are not "black and white," or "mutually exclusive!" Just because this is called "Duty-Based Orientation" doesn't in any way mean you don't get a lot of pleasure and joy out of it!

Not at all. To the contrary, your feeling of joy and wellbeing and positive sense of whom you are—all wonderful and deeply satisfying feelings—can most definitely be part of the Duty-Based Orientation, and frequently are.

It's just that pleasure is not the be-all and end-all of WHY you do something, is it?

If your Marriage Blueprint is based on "Duty Based Orientation," these are some of the things you prize very highly in a marriage:

(Remember that the Pleasure-Oriented person can value these also, but to you they are so prominent and important that **you can't imagine a good marriage without them**)

- Fierce loyalty and dedication to the marriage and to one another
- Rules or guidance by which to live life together that are followed
- Accomplishment and achievement as measured by standards
- Consistency and focus
- Longevity in marriage. You admire long lasting marriages very much.

**To you it makes no sense to even call it a marriage if there aren't guidelines to follow or basic principles that you live by.**

You most definitely can have fun and enjoy yourself, but it tends to be *"Work first, play later."* In reality (and you can be misunderstood about this), work itself is very enjoyable, partly because of the powerful sense of accomplishment it brings, but also because work in itself is pleasurable.

It seems amazing to you that so many people live their lives in a kind of "catch as catch can" way, just improvising as they go along through life and marriage and family.

### "If only others would follow a plan"

You believe that everyone's marriage and family life could be greatly improved and satisfying if they would just get a plan and follow it! What's so hard about that? All they need is to follow a system and the guidelines within it, and they can be much more settled and calm.

It's clear to you within marriage, just as in other areas of life, *everything works better with structure.* Maybe you don't perfectly follow the "Seven Habits of Highly Successfully People," but you readily see their value and believe that the more closely you follow them the more successful you will be.

**You really admire long-term marriages,** and have a lot of respect for what you think is their ability to "overcome differences and hardships." That kind of thinking appeals to you very much, and feels very heroic and meaningful to you.

**As a matter of fact, you generally admire "heroism" in anybody and any situation.** If someone risks their life for another person or endures sacrifice, if they undergo pain and massive challenges to overcome, they get your attention and admiration.

The Biblical Job, who remained faithful to God even when all of his possessions were taken away, he lost his wealth and his family and his own personal health and still praised God, is a model to you because he stayed steadfast in his devotion and commitment.

You really admire commitment to a purpose, and keeping a vow—even if it is in the light of great temptation and sacrifice.

Marriage to you might not always be "fun" or "all a bed of roses," but you are not put off by that, because you know to expect it (and of course, that's what you get since "The Marriage That You Have Is the Marriage You Expect To Have!").

**You think of yourself as a "realist" who understands life "as it really is."** You think of yourself as a person who tirelessly tries to follow your greatest values, and possibly be a good influence on others.

You may have been the kind of kid that parents of your girlfriend or boyfriend really wanted her/him to hang out with: responsible, loyal, and dependable.

You are the kind of person that my farm relatives used to say, "He'll close the gates," meaning that if you went into a field to hunt or fish, you would close the gates so the livestock wouldn't get out.

Dependability is something that you prize in marriage and elsewhere, and it gives you a good feeling when people say that about you.

For the most part, you see that the purpose of duty in marriage and family life is to get outside of your own self and be of service and use to others. And to help them achieve the life that they themselves are called to live.

Your Marriage Blueprint calls for service to a set of guidelines, whether more secular (law, social conventions, order) or more theological (the Biblical Law, the Koran, the Eight Noble Truths).

The more closely you are living to those guidelines, the calmer and greater sense of wellbeing you tend to have.

Here's the way you tend to look at these parts of marriage and family life if you have a Duty-Based Marriage Blueprint:

## Sex

Sex is an extremely important part of married life to you (and probably only to married life or at least to a committed relationship, to your way of believing), but not something to be taken lightly.

It can be of wonderful joy and pleasure, as long as it is serving a greater purpose, whether to glorify the Divine and Holy in your marriage, or for the purpose of bringing children into the world.

You would prefer using the phrase "making love"—because just to call it "sex" or to use other more *gutter-terms* sounds like it's just an animal function with no meaning. You prefer to think of things people do as meaning something—and this goes for sex as much as anything else.

Your duty is to follow the guidelines you have about sex, faithfulness and love.

## Parenting and Kids

You have a job to do with your children, which is to bring them up with *standards!* This is your most important "first line" job as a parent, and your Marriage Blueprint calls for you to be a very faithful and devoted leader to your children.

Children are wonderful and appreciated and loved, but you need to be careful not to let your sentiments or empathy get in the way of giving them the discipline they need in order to have a productive and purposeful life.

Duty and accomplishment are more important in the end than fun, so it's homework first, then the playing, and to bed on time, because if they get used to getting their way, they will have no inner discipline.

Marriage is a big part of the stability of the family, and it is your duty and your spouse's duty to create stability and security, so that your children can grow up feeling secure, confident and strong, so they can carry on in a similar way to you in their lives. You are their model and however responsible and consistent you are is how much you can expect them to be.

## Money

Money is used first of all for family security and stability, according to your Marriage Blueprint.

Your Marriage Blueprint calls for saving, prioritizing and budgeting. You may or may not DO very well with these areas, but your Belief System calls for making sure that whatever goes out is for a reason and cause that serves your values, and that you are doing the right thing, and in the right way.

You are goal-oriented in relation to your money. Perhaps you don't fully fulfill your goals all the time, but you believe you should. You are keenly aware of the need for goals for such things as retirement, and you feel a strong drive to meet those goals to define yourself as a success.

## Personal Development

Personal development is primarily for improvement in serving your goals and doing your duty.

If you go for further education, it is to help you reach those goals. If you go to a seminar, read a book, watch a video, it's best if it is related to fulfilling your goals and values. Doesn't HAVE to be, but it is preferable.

Sure, you can take a vacation and completely get away and play with the best of them, but play should come as a reward for hard work and something you have earned!

You believe that the more you and your partner develop in your discipline and ability to reach your goals individually, and as a couple, the stronger your marriage will be.

Your Marriage Blueprint calls for a marriage which is to be admired and respected for its strength, consistency, longevity, and integrity according to the guidelines you live by.

## Religion and Spirituality

One of the purposes of a religion, according to your Blueprint, is to give you guidelines and standards by which you can measure yourself.

This may or may not be a traditional religion, that's not the point to you.

The point is whether the religion or organization can give you guidelines that you respect, and that if you follow them, you can gain respect yourself.

Your view of yourself and others in your family and in your marriage is "conditional." By that I mean that others—and you even more—are measured against standards. The more they or you meet the standards, the higher "rank" you deserve.

Your worth is based at least in mortal human terms on your achieved merit!

# CHAPTER NINETEEN

## ME or WE?
### Two "Styles"—Independence V. Joining Preference

**Independence Preference Versus Joining Preference**

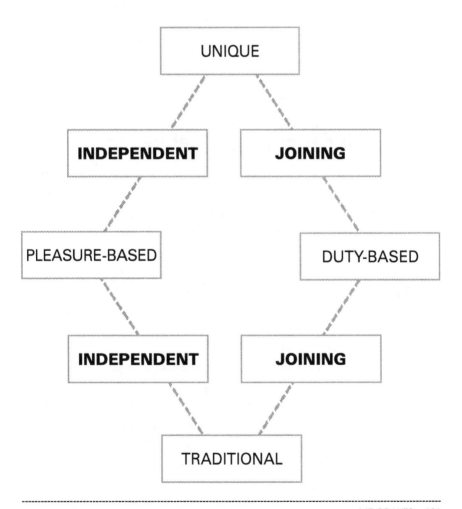

OVERLAID on the Four Points (Pleasure v. Duty and Uniqueness v. Tradition) is what I call a preference for either Independence or Joining.

**Reminder:** these are "tendencies" and that they are rarely found in the purest 100% form. So don't be surprised at all if you find some aspects of pleasure and some of duty in your Marriage Blueprint—or in your own preferences!

Now we will add the final dimension to the Marriage Blueprints and how they work. We have one more thing to add, which is "Styles." These Styles are connected to the Directions to create a complete Marriage Blueprint!

Styles refers to two separate and somewhat opposite factors in a Marriage Blueprint. I call the two "Styles" Independence and Joining. Let me explain. In brief, independence emphasizes the individual within the marriage as first in priority; joining emphasizes the connection within the marriage as first in priority.

Which do you *emphasize?* Let's find out.

# Independence Preference

In this "Style" of Marriage Blueprint, one of the **most highly prized** and valued principle of a Great Marriage is the principle of **independence or autonomy of the individuals within the marriage.**

With "Independence," the main thing is *BEING AN INDIVIDUAL.*

This doesn't necessarily mean that people with the "Independence Style" have a view of "disconnection" or "detachment." Not at all!

If you have this Style, you emphasize that people, in order to become truly connected, have to have a powerful sense of their own individuality—and own personal sense of self—before they can even possibly experience intimacy.

**Some people put it this way. "In order to love you, I must love me first." That's the Independence Style.**

The Independence Style, which is one shared by a lot of psychologists, is the strongly held view that each partner needs to become "differentiated," or self-actualized as an individual in order to create the possibility of a true sharing of selves in marriage.

If you have a strong "Independence" Style in your Marriage Blueprint, you are likely to **emphasize:**

- **Self understanding** and **self acceptance** as a *prerequisite* to Great Marriage and intimacy
- The extreme importance of **individual responsibility** in Marriage
- *A "contractual" view of marriage as an agreement between individuals*
- The same rights, privileges, responsibilities and freedoms that I expect should be extended to my partner as well.

Again, it's not that the person with the "other" Style ("Joining") wouldn't agree with these things, it's that if you have this Style, you **emphasize them.**

They are first priority to you.

You see Independence as the Horse and Joining as the Cart.

Independence comes first.

Being your own person is seen as a great virtue in these descriptions. If you have an "Independence Style" Marriage Blueprint, you'll find yourself *STRONGLY* agreeing with the spirit of these descriptions.

## Independents Reject "Enmeshment"

Also, from the literature of "Independence Style" writings, comes a strong criticism of the other style, which is "Joining"-often seen by the Independents in its most negative form, where it is called "enmeshment."

**Independents REALLY like their individuality, and they don't like anybody or anything messing with it!**

These are comments about "enmeshment" and the views of different individuals about the effects of "enmeshment," which is identified as a form of "Joining" which usurps and harms individuals within relationships.

- Some have said that enmeshment is attempting to feel and think as if you were the same person.
- Others have said that enmeshment is a transactional style where family members are highly involved with one another, but **it's suffocating.**
- Others have said that enmeshment is disguised as support and friendship when it truly is *only manipulation.*

- Others have said that enmeshment is important for a relationship, but with time, **hurt and disappointment set in and the process becomes toxic.**
- Others have said that enmeshment is there to remind you that you are never separate from the other person ultimately, and **deny you your individuality.**
- Others have said that enmeshment is the same as the **relationship addiction** called co-dependence.
- Others have said that enmeshment is like being caught in an *emotional net from which there seems to be no escape.*
- Others have said that enmeshment is the **inappropriate closeness** of family members against a backdrop, of course, of developmental appropriateness.

Obviously,"enmeshment" is clearly something these independents don't like. "Smothering, toxic, suffocating, inappropriate, addiction." Some very strong language there. So you can see that the "Independence" Style wouldn't want anything they felt was "suffocating" getting anywhere near to them!

AIR, PLEASE!

If you identify with these statements, it is more than likely that the whole process of **extreme "joining"** in relationships has a distaste—or a history of negative connotation—for you.

**If so, you should know that the very things you find "suffocating" or "smothering" someone else might feel was very comforting, recharging, enjoyable and delightful!**

All I am saying here is that if you have the "Independence Style" in your Marriage Blueprint, be careful about thinking that it should universally apply to others!

You might have the belief that people being "his or her own person" is a very good thing as an essential and extremely strong component of your Marriage Blueprint, but someone else (such as your spouse) **MAY NOT.**

Your spouse might have a strong "Joining" style, and given your "Independence Style" guidelines, you are obliged to give this person the latitude to have his own style—**that is, if you expect to generate understanding and respect in your marriage.**

Also, you should do a gut check to make certain that your Independence-Style is based on solid and true principles of your Belief, and not only on Defensiveness, because you are afraid to get as close to another person as you really long to be (and your Marriage Blueprint actually calls for).

# The "Joining" Style

"No man is an island," say these folks, and they wouldn't want to be an island if they could!

If your Marriage Blueprint calls for a "Joining Style," you have a **strong emphasis** on togetherness, family, group energy, and interdependence of one person on another.

### "WE-ness"

In your Blueprint, each individual is truly part of the whole—the marriage or the family—and togetherness or "we-ness" is the high ideal. When your marriage or family has that sense of powerful "we-ness" or what I call "Joining," you feel a real sense of wellbeing!

You (Joining Style folks) know and understand from your belief system that the whole is stronger than the parts, and that **everyone is lifted up by the health, joy and wellbeing of the whole.** That is to say, if you and I work together—and don't put so much emphasis on our own individual ego or personal reactions, but instead on our mutual happiness—we will both be happier from our cooperation and synergy of connection.

You believe in "a rising tide floats all boats," and "if everyone is not happy (wealthy, well-fed, physically healthy), I'm not." You pray for the wellbeing of all of us!

Here are some descriptions about "Joining" which may convey some of this feeling:

- Joining is shared in the intimate areas of your lives where it really counts, and it's about truly **being together without ego.**
- Joining is important to maintaining marital satisfaction in every stage of life. *The more together and connected we are around common causes the happier the marriage will ultimately be.*

We both need to relinquish our egos to the happiness of the marriage and family.

- **Joining is the preferred way of being in a relationship because it allows everyone to participate in the benefits!**
- Joining is both new and yet feels like it has been there always; when we discover that there really is not a thing as "just you" or "just me" but **we are connected permanently and deeply, it feels like it's been that way forever.**
- Joining is the defining characteristic of marriage; if you want individuality, be single!

A friend of mine, Nate, opened a mission in Nigeria whose purpose is to make sure that everyone gets proper nourishment. He believes that you have to start on the true level of sharing of the goods of the earth for all our salvations. In his words, **he believes that "If one person on earth is starving, we are all starving." He believes that ultimately the salvation of each of us depends on the salvation of all of us!**

He's a true model of a "Joiner!"

Most of us wouldn't think to live by the same standards as Nate—they are too extreme. However, you may think he is right in spirit. If you agree with him, and feel that is the underlying principle you should be following in your life (specifically in your marriage), then your Style is Joining!

However, your spouse may have a very different view about these questions. He or she may prefer the Independence Style, and it is your obligation if you want intimacy to find 100% acceptance. After all, you value Joining very deeply, and if you are going to generate a spirit of joining and connection with your spouse, you will most definitely wish to accept your spouse's Independence style to deepen that connection and intimacy.

## Quick Review of the Marriage Blueprint Map

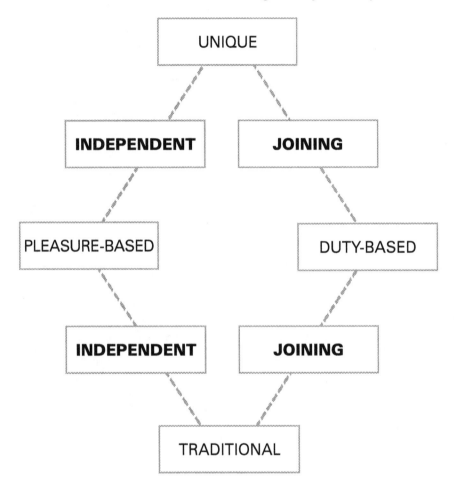

Now we have two Styles:
- Independence
- Joining

Which we are going to join with Four Directions in Two Poles
- Unique versus
- Traditional

And
- Pleasure Based versus
- Duty Based

---

# CHAPTER TWENTY

## The 8 Marriage Blueprints
### Solve Your Intimacy Paradox!

These Blueprints are combinations of the ingredients of Directions and Styles. They describe in general terms a basic picture of 8 different "Marriage Blueprint" types.

### Questions You Should Be Asking

As you are reading the descriptions of these 8 Marriage Blueprints, you should be asking yourself these questions:

1. What is my "Family" Marriage Blueprint—which of these 8 is the closest to my own earliest version of what marriage is—and what it should be?

2. What is my "Personal" Marriage Blueprint—which of these 8 is the closest to what I NOW think marriage is, and what it should be?

3. What is my spouse's "Family" Marriage Blueprint—which of these 8 is the closest to his or her own earliest version of what marriage is—and what it should be?

4. What is my spouse's "Personal" Marriage Blueprint—which of these 8 is the closest to what he or she NOW thinks marriage is—and what it should be?

5. Which of these 8 is the closest description of the Marriage we are ACTUALLY LIVING RIGHT NOW?

6. How close or far away from the two Blueprints I have for mar-

riage is the marriage we are actually living right now? How true is this marriage to what I expect and think it should be?

7. How close or far away from the two Blueprints my partner has for marriage is the marriage we are actually living right now? How true is this marriage to what he or she expects and thinks it should be?

As you read about the 8 Marriage Blueprints, keep these questions in mind. At the end of the book, you'll find my free bonus to do an online evaluation to help you if you have trouble deciding which Blueprint fits you best.

One thing you might find amazing, as many of my clients have found. In just reading these descriptions, you may find that your marriage is changing positively. It could feel like a miracle. Spontaneous change is possible!

Do you believe that a Great Marriage or any other wonderful thing can be spontaneously generated by a true insight and Belief System change?

---

### The 8 Marriage Blueprints

For each of these, I am going to give you a "snapshot" of the Marriage Blueprint, and then how this Marriage Blueprint "shows up" in the areas of Sex, Parenting, Money, Personal Development and Religion/Spirituality in the marriage and family.

---

1. "Wild Things" page

2. "Bliss-Mates" page

3. "Pilgrims" page

4. "The Big Heart Family" page

5. "Pioneers" page

6. "The Visionary Family" page

7. "The Golden Rule Family" page

8. "The Royal Family" page

## 1. "Wild Things!"

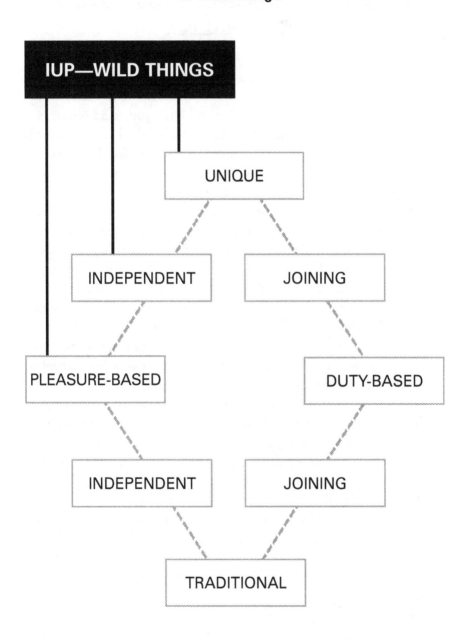

# Independent Unique Pleasure-Based Blueprint: IUP

Couple's favorite theme song? Maybe *"Wild Thing (I think I love you)."*

Hey, if you are "Wild Things," you are probably going to think that my descriptions of you are far too tame, that I've understated the power and excitement of who you are and what you stand for.

Even to say "who you are" may make you bristle. How dare I even try to describe you? You are too dynamic to be described! You are like the Shape Shifters of Native American stories, who could be human, then eagle, then coyote, as circumstances required.

Maybe "Shape-Shifters" would be a better term for you. No? Well, I tried. Let me try to say a few things about you to others who aren't like you, and see if I can increase their understanding of you, and if I can help others see that your way of living is just as valid as theirs, you have just as much reason to call yours a marriage as they do.

This Marriage Blueprint may seem odd to many people, and **possibly not even like any kind of marriage** as we commonly think about it. There's a lot of societal pressure against this kind of marriage, because it is so far away from the statistical norm of most people's marriages, and from their definition of the "ideal marriage."

The theme of this "Wild Things" marriage is "parallel pleasure." Each person in the marriage model is seeking *his or her own personal pleasure and fun,* and doing it in **his or her own way, without restrictions imposed or expected.** As a matter of fact, extremely little is expected if anything at all from one another in this marriage.

If you were in this marriage, what you would expect?

You'd expect that both you and your partner would be *constantly seeking new experiences, according to your own individual paths,* and that you may very well not see your partner for a while, and that they *might just "be gone" at a moment's notice,* doing something of interest or passion.

*But that's cool, no problem!*

"Rules" as such don't really exist in this Marriage Blueprint. The only rule is that "there are no rules," except that newness, excitement, pleasure—on the individual level—is the pattern of life that you have.

No sexual jealousy or other kinds of possessiveness, or demands on one another are accepted as part of this picture.

If you have the "Wild Things" (IUP) as your Marriage Blueprint, you expect that marriage holds no constriction on your freedom, but instead fundamentally encourages and supports the seeking of individual pleasure and dynamic changes.

This Marriage Blueprint is consistent with what is often called the "Gestalt Prayer" by Fritz Perls in 1969.

> I do my thing and you do your thing.
> I am not in this world to live up to your expectations,
> And you are not in this world to live up to mine.
> You are you, and I am I,
> And if by chance we find each other, it's beautiful.
> If not, it can't be helped.
> —*Fritz Perls, 1969*

### Sex

There are no true rules if you are a "real" IUP, except that you owe your partner the same freedom you have. Your sexual habits and interests—each of you as individuals—are your own and not subject to control, criticism or questioning by your partner.

In this marriage, any form of sexual experimentation is "within bounds," and is considered a potential source of growth and development, the cardinal elements of a "Great Marriage" as defined by this Marriage Blueprint.

**You are free, and owe your partner freedom.** The only guideline is that if you attempt to restrict the freedom of the other person, you have committed a foul!

### Parenting and Kids

If you are an IUP, your view of parenting is to encourage the same ideals of discovery and individual experimentation in your children that you encourage in yourself and in one another.

In other words, the job you have as a parent is to make certain that your child is exposed to as many new and different sources of pleasure, passion and curiosity as you possibly can, and for the child to be the truest individual person he or she can be.

You support and encourage individualism, uniqueness and pleasure above all other values. You value individual freedom and creativity above all other things, according to this Marriage Blueprint, so why wouldn't you encourage and even require your children to do the same?

You see life—marriage, family and your individual life—as fully up to the individual and his or her unique passions. All is built upon and developed from this personal passion. Discovery and experimentation are goals in themselves, and need no more explaining.

You are going to expose your children to all kinds of ways of living, and give them a chance to explore as much as they possibly can, to discover more and more what is of interest to them.

## Money

**Money is generated for the purpose of funding your individual discoveries, passions, and interests!**

You expect to have enough money and time to pursue your passions, and for your partner to have enough money to pursue his or hers also (and the kids, too).

Money is not there to be saved "for a rainy day," but to be used to have experiences today!

*You never know if you'll be here tomorrow.*

You are free to make and spend as you like, as your partner is. If for example, you find yourself without money or terribly in debt, that also could be interesting and a source of learning and discovery. "No problem!"

On the other hand, you might be very conscientious in your money-making and saving efforts—but for the purpose of acquiring enough money that each of you can pursue perhaps very expensive interests.

## Personal Development: Individual Discovery!

Your Marriage Blueprint calls for exploration, discovery and following your passions, so *personal INDIVIDUAL development* (unless you and your partner just happen to be interested in the same things) is going to occur, and expected to happen at a good clip—and to go on indefinitely.

In any case, since uniqueness is called for, you are likely to find your own special interests that will help you stand out, or be the representative of something different, new, and powerful—and that the world may never have seen before.

Your own interests, whether in sports, academics, sewing, exotic shopping, sexual adventure, travel, model railroads, movies, fishing and hunting, art—or whatever it happens to be—are to be followed, and your partner is expected to have the same freedom to follow his or hers (kids, too).

**Whatever it is, you are going to find your own unique version of it.**

### Religion and Spirituality: *A Unique, Personalized Slant*

Spirituality definitely is likely to be a part of your landscape and expressed interests, although formal religion is very unlikely to be your "cup of tea."

You and your partner might have some of the same religious/spiritual pursuits, but it won't be required or expected. Nor are you *required or expected* to continue on the same pathway for any longer than you like.

You are driven by pleasure and your own interests. You are unlikely to ever follow any strict religious path, but if you do, it will be to see how you react and you will consider it an "adventure of discovery."

If you do belong to a religious organization, it's more than likely to be pretty far out of the mainstream, and maybe out of the stream altogether, or alternatively, even if you are involved in formal religious practice, you are going to participate in such a way that will probably disrupt the church, temple or mosque you belong to. *You'll be asking that heretical word "Why?"* far too often for most people.

### STRENGTHS

The IUP, "Wild Things" Marriage Blueprint generates exciting, dynamic marriages!

They are very alive, and always full of interesting *new stories, adventures and possibilities.* Those who live (and survive) inside of those relationships are usually very interesting, story-filled personalities.

*The children of IUP marriages are some of the most creative, unique and unusual kids you'll meet.* Often their views about the world and people are quite fresh, and even amazing.

With their views about money, *sometimes people in IUP Marriages end up shockingly or staggeringly wealthy.* Since they are willing to take chances in life and "go outside the norms," they can come up with surprising resources and creative methods to make money in ways that most people would not have thought of.

In the realm of creativity, spirituality, religion, education, IUP family members can sometimes generate the most unexpected and unforeseen new inventions or ideas, because they are not looking in the same places as other people.

IUP marriages can work, and do work among certain people with dramatic and sparkling results, even though to most of us that have "quieter, more standard" marriages, these IUP marriages can seem so weird and different that we can't imagine how they could succeed, or even that they can be classified as marriages at all.

Another area where you can see that it's not profitable to pre-judge, without living inside of someone's head and life, whether the choices they have made are "good" or "bad."

## Challenges

IUP marriages face potential termination through eventual changes that are so radical that the individuals in the marriage no longer even "know each other," like they once did. But people who have IUP Marriage Blueprints would say, as in the Gestalt Prayer, "It can't be helped."

So we could say that "stability" or "longevity" are challenges, but would they care?

It can be sometimes that the IUP Marriage Blueprint is a Personal Marriage Blueprint that is not workable for a person with a far different Family Marriage Blueprint. From this perspective, it is not much more than an attractive opportunity to try on a dynamic and interesting lifestyle, but not something a person wants to live in forever.

**However, there are people who do live out of the IUP Marriage Blueprint as a perfectly natural part of who they are.** One challenge for them is that, in life there are sometimes mishaps that do literally debilitate us to the point where we need nursing or other medical care, and the IUP doesn't call for anyone to be there to provide it.

But to the person with a strong and consistent IUP Marriage Blueprint, this may very well not even be taken as a problem. Friends of mine, Jason and Marie, have lived this IUP world as a married couple for 23 years. They are getting older, and Marie had a cancer scare (she called it *"interesting"*) several months ago.

What she said was that she "wouldn't be debilitated or in nursing home," that she would "be gone far before that." She didn't say, but I felt that she was saying she'd rather be dead than live without her health and freedom. A powerful statement on her part, and in her case, one I believe is genuine and upon which I wouldn't be surprised if she acted.

So people with IUP Marriage Blueprints could have issues to solve as they age or become debilitated, and it's possible even at a young age, since the "Wild Things" tend to go for things which could be life threatening.

**But then again, they might not have problems, ever! Their spirit of adventure, discovery and individual independence may allow them some ways of meeting those challenges that are truly "unique," and that they will design on their own, and out of their vast, accumulated, directly-experienced wisdom about life.**

To many people, their "unsettled" ways of living and "uncertain" financial, emotional and familial life looks tiring, confusing and fear provoking. Those who truly live the IUP Marriage Blueprint, however, claim that it is none of those, but rather exhilarating, clear and very interesting, and that they don't feel fear but excitement about these challenges.

After all, they are "Wild Things!"

---

## FACING THE CHALLENGE:

Since all Great Marriages are based on 100% acceptance of self and 100% acceptance of your spouse, your challenge is:

1. To **stay connected** and feel like you belong with a family and others. You are so individualistic that even though people find you appealing and interesting, many people may just follow your lead and neither ask nor require anything of you. *Friendships for most people are built on mutual help and*

*obligation,* and though you don't like that, you might find yourself quite alone at some time, and might find that very painful.

2. You have a *tendency to burn bridges* with other people, not
   because of any intention to hurt on your part, but because
   other people might be more sensitive to being hurt than you.
   *It might surprise you* that they could react so strongly, but
   remember that YOU are the one who is different from others.

## IF THIS IS YOUR PREFERRED MARRIAGE BLUEPRINT AND YOUR SPOUSE HAS ANOTHER PREFFERED MARRIAGE BLUEPRINT:

1. Your spouse might seem "boring" to you at times, and it could
   be quite a challenge for you to accept his or her difference
   from you; but you should be "up to the challenge," since you
   like challenges!

2. Your tendency to always be "mixing it up" and exploring *may
   lead you* to miss some of the wonderful benefits you might get
   from slowing down and focusing. Many of the other
   Blueprints offer powerful benefits that you might miss. Watch
   carefully for what you can learn from other ways of being married!

These answers to your challenges are meant as a "starter kit" for
you in how to handle differences or conflicts between you and your
spouse, or even conflicts inside of you between competing Marriage
Blueprints! For more discussion and to get all your questions
answered, please visit www.CouplesCoach.com .

## 2. "Blissmates™"

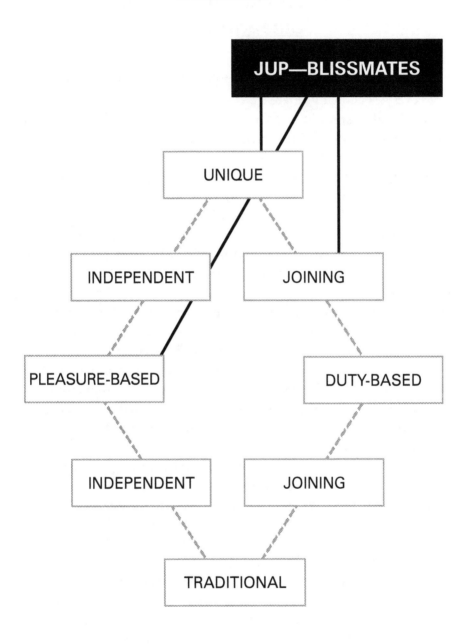

# Joined Unique Pleasure-Based Blueprint: JUP

Theme: "Let's go exploring, together!"

Like the "Wild Things," the "Blissmates" exist for pleasure and discovery! The main difference is that the focus is much less on the "individual" expression of uniqueness and pleasure seeking, and much more on the "joined" search for uniqueness and pleasure.

Those with the JUP are also very lively, but they are doing all their exploring, experimenting, discovery and seeking **together.** And that's exactly how they like it and want it.

If you are "Blissmates," you know it. I don't have to say much more to you about what you like and how you operate, as a matter of fact, probably just after you read the term "Blissmates," you probably took off for some kind of adventure, and aren't even here reading anymore! ☺ *Bon voyage!*

So I'll just talk to the other people about you because most people misunderstand you anyway. They think you are irresponsible, unreliable, a bit crazy and mysterious (they might just be jealous).

If the couple has no children, then the two of them will explore together as a couple. "Exploration" can mean anything from travel and experiencing events in the world to "inner work" that that the couple does together—which might involve meditation, prayer, or a whole range of creative methods of discovery.

If the couple with the "Blissmates" (JUP) marriage are spiritual seekers, they will have looked together at many "portals of discovery" after a few years. Those might include even occult methods such as Tarot, astrology and other realms of study, or they might be involved in a "standard church, temple or mosque," but are practicing their own very unique version of the practice.

The Blissmates couple may have explored sexually with other couples and other genders as a couple; they might have traveled to exotic places on a lark; they may have started a company with a highly speculative product and possibly either "went platinum" or "went bust;" they might have home schooled their children in Latin; they might have made their living panning gold and found enough nuggets to move to Costa Rica for a year; they may have invented a new way to carry babies; or "imported" (smuggled) diamonds from Africa; but whatever they have done, you can bet it was something that unless you are a Blissmates couple yourself, you probably didn't do or perhaps didn't even think about doing.

### Sex

As I said, the couple with the "Blissmates" Marriage Blueprint has no particular restrictions on sexuality or its expression, because it involves discovery and pleasure; but unlike the "Wild Things" couple they did their sexual explorations together.

They might potentially be a "statistically odd" couple, such as a bisexual man and a heterosexual woman or any other combination, but this "nomenclature" doesn't mean a thing to them as long as they are experimenting or discovering as a couple. This couple might not marry at all, but will live a life as a married couple.

But I don't want to give the wrong impression. The Blissmates couple might look or seem extremely "ordinary," and yet their own sense of adventure and excitement and discovery could be very powerful and driving.

"Joined" is a big word to them, as is "unique"—the pleasure seeking just seems natural, and they couldn't imagine a life without it.

If you are a Blissmates couple, your relationship may get more "out there" than most peoples'—because you have such a strong craving and longing for togetherness and exploring together. Highs and lows? Potentially far more extreme than most people's.

But because of your dedication to exploring and learning the truth, you will not only go places emotionally and intellectually— and literally that other people don't "dare to tread"—but you also will find the tools to handle the challenges that come up when you get there!

Thanks for taking the lead in showing us all what is *possible out there on the frontier*—even if most of us aren't going to go there.

It's nice to dream, and you help us do it!

---

## Parenting and Kids

Blissmates find kids wonderful, although some Blissmates couples don't want even "wonderful" kids to be part of their world, since kids can be "restrictive" to discovery.

The couple with the JUP Marriage Blueprint is likely to either have children of their own or look to spend time with children of friends, neighbors or relatives.

This is because "joining" is very important to them, as is exploring and learning. *They enjoy the unusual and amazing things that children add to life.* They might adopt, or participate in a children's shelter or educational program.

When it comes to parenting, the Blissmates couple wants to provide fun and enjoyment, discovery and excitement for their children. To many of us, it may seem that they put their children in more jeopardy than we would find prudent.

The Blissmates couple tries to provide experiences for their children where the kids can learn from unique, extraordinary or special means. Their children are likely to have traveled or spent time in places where most kids have never been, nor have their parents even thought about taking them. As such, they can be considered "interesting and appealing" to other kids, or alternately, as "weird and geeky," and may be ostracized from other kids.

Their parents are proud of these unique kids, and it's almost true that the "weirder" other kids think they are, the "prouder" the parents in the Blissmates couple will be of them.

## Money

Money in the "Blissmates" Marriage Blueprint serves for "family fun and exploration."

The Blissmates family will *always find resources* to do things that might seem impossible to outside families. It might look like they don't have any money at all, and suddenly the whole family is on a plane to Chile where they are going to work at a fly-fishing lodge for two years—or even are going to "buy it." How? No one seems to know, but there they go!

The Blissmates family *learns a tremendous kind of resourcefulness* because of their focus on "joining" and working together as a team to seek pleasure, enjoyment and discovery. They really do "join" their heads together to get the results they want. *No one is left out, and they can miraculously include everyone.*

Even when nothing seems to work for them, and no money has come in for a long time, they will continuously come up with "the goods." Might even be from criminal activity, might just as easily be from some very creative use of talents and energies that suddenly gushers-open a money well to them!

### Personal Development

For the Blissmates couple, personal development is a very high value; and yet it's usually undertaken as a couple, not individually. Might not look like it. Jane takes art classes, Larry goes to school at the same time and takes a literature class, and thus they both find something interesting to do, and the endeavors and activities are almost the same!

If one has a challenge that comes up (such as an illness, a difficult exam, a job demand, a new project that has to be completed in record time) the other is immediately involved, and is expected to be involved. *There's no gap between the problem and the joining of the two to solve it.*

They'll come up with a unique solution, but if it becomes unpleasant or uninteresting, they both might decide to shelve the whole thing, and gather the family together to go to Yellowstone National Park instead. ☺

To most of us they would appear erratic or chaotic, but maybe it's jealousy! In your heart of hearts, wouldn't you rather just sideline all the difficulties around you and take off on a great trip and have fun together?

No? If you said "No," that's a sure-fire indication you are not a "Blissmates" couple!

### Religion and Spirituality

Blissmates couples are driven in their spirituality by pleasure and discovery!

If you are a Blissmates couple, you probably have some special spiritual "secrets" because of your explorations together—and we look forward to your next book or seminar where you will reveal all to us, that is if you have time between explorations, or don't get too bored writing the book!

Blissmates are much more likely to *start* a church than to join one, and, as a matter of fact, if you go to their house, you are likely to find out that they have done exactly that. The "Unique" part of their blueprint calls for them to find the "truth behind the truth."

They might have altars encompassing several religions, combining elements they liked from each (never anything that they don't like or find appealing). As a matter of fact, they could just as easily be living in an old converted church, and be doing their own religious ceremonies right on the old altar in that church, or not. Don't think you'll be able to predict or control what a Blissmates family does.

## *STRENGTHS* of the Blissmates Marriage

Togetherness and joining help compensate for the fact that this couple or family may regularly be "out on a limb!"-they will usually stay together, even though occasionally things "get a little weird."

Working together, having a Belief System that encourages incredible group synergy and group problem solving, this might very well be the most extraordinary couple or family you'll ever meet.

They might make you a little nervous, though!

This can be a very LOUD, boisterous and energetic family! It might seem like a display of utter chaos!

They are not likely to be like anyone else you've ever met. Their solutions to the usual "life problems" we all face are often so different and so unique that they could make your head spin.

Always interesting, though always somewhat intense, the JUP couple is entertaining and never without a story, a new idea, a new possibility they are hatching, and usually never without some kinds of challenges which might make others extremely nervous: no money, no place to live (didn't they used to have that great house up on Lilac Lane?), or potentially a law suit on their ledger that hasn't been solved.

But they seem to always come up with answers to everything. They are models of what we call "resourceful" in the most generous and happy use of that term.

## Challenges of the Blissmates (JUP) Marriage Blueprint

Sometimes, however, answers don't come for a while, even to the most resourceful people. They may come, but there might be long periods of time that can involve suffering, loss and even danger.

If you are a Blissmates kind of person, I can hear you licking your chops at this. "Oh, but it's *exciting! Isn't so much of life BORING otherwise?*" Most of the rest of us are much more concerned about safety and security than whether we might sometimes be bored!

The Blissmates family *may always be living on "the edge," financially, socially, potentially even legally.* They **take chances** that to them seem just as their own answers to things. And sometimes they might have the view of themselves as a little "above the law."

Talking to other like-minded people sometimes can convince you that being on the edge is OK because other people appear to have calibrated the "edge" at too normal or boring or mediocre a place.

So they can sometimes be in trouble—or just about to be in trouble.

But the Blissmates couple is resourceful, so most of the time they will figure out how to get out of a jam, or even how to turn the jam into a positive situation—even a wonderful and powerful opportunity. Not only "When one door closes, another opens," like most of us finally realize in a philosophical way, but the Blissmates couple *frankly just can't* wait until this current (now gone stale) door closes, so they can get on to the next door!

Follow-through to "fulfilling potential" is NOT top priority with the Blissmates couple! They'd rather get on with the new opportunity!

Children of Blissmates Marriages may feel very confused and unsettled at times, and maybe even feel that they are in danger a lot. They might be seen by Blissmates parents as being "too sensitive," and exhorted to "get over it." However, since the establishment of Belief Systems, as I have showed you, is unique to each individual; sometimes children don't fit at all into a Blissmates marriage.

And sometimes one of the marriage partners gets fed up with the JUP lifestyle. Perhaps it was not really his or her Family Marriage Blueprint to begin with, or perhaps the constant development and emphasis on change and development has led him or her to develop a new Personal Marriage Blueprint that doesn't fit with this JUP version.

## FACING THE CHALLENGE:

Since all Great Marriages are based on 100% acceptance of self and 100% acceptance of your spouse, your challenge is:

1. Your dedication to being Blissmates is so intense and strong that it could be a problem for your spouse if he or she gets tired of the intensity, or it doesn't match their own energy level. **You could feel very disappointed or let down by this.** What you should do instead is just take a break, and let your partner rest. Insisting on intensity when your spouse is resting or taking a break, may have the unintended consequences of driving her or him away! Just the opposite of what you would like. **So be careful with your intensity.**

2. Your intense focus on one another in the marriage may cut you off from others in your life (family, friends, co-workers), so that **they may feel alienated by you two.** If having friends is important to you, you might try to realize that most of the rest of the world is less intense than you, and in order to relate to others you can put some understanding into their points of view.

## IF THIS IS YOUR PREFERRED MARRIAGE BLUEPRINT AND YOUR SPOUSE HAS ANOTHER PREFFERED MARRIAGE BLUEPRINT:

1. If your spouse prefers another Marriage Blueprint, this can be *very trying, and even potentially very depressing to you.* You could feel betrayed by what you **perceive as their rejection of you—** because of their unwillingness or low interest in an intense "Blissmate" way of life with you. Handling this **difference could be a huge challenge,** and you might need some help "translating" your spouse's intentions to you, so that you don't conclude they are "betraying you."

2. Alternatively, you may need some help "translating" your own intensity and desires to your spouse, since he or she might see your push to be "Blissmates" as *invasive or suffocating—**not your intention, but your spouse may see it this way.*** Carefully formulate your way of helping your spouse see what it is you are about, and what you really want. Be thoughtful, and he or she might end up seeing the whole thing differently.

These answers to your challenges are meant as a "starter kit" for you in how to handle differences or conflicts between you and your spouse, or even conflicts inside of you between competing Marriage Blueprints! For more discussion and to get all your questions answered, please visit www.CouplesCoach.com

### 3. "Pilgrims"

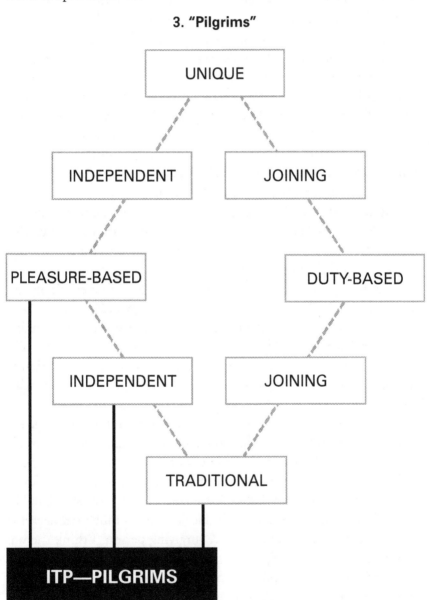

# Independent-Traditional-Pleasure-Based Blueprint: ITP

Twenty years ago my friend Marilyn decided to take three months off work to follow in the footsteps of the medieval pilgrims of Spain, on what is called El *Camino de Santiago de Compostela.*

During the Middle Ages, since the 12th century, hundreds of thousands (or millions) of people have trekked across Northern Spain along the Pyrenees from east to west on a spiritual journey—on foot—to the Holy Shrine at Santiago de Compostela, at the far northwest corner of Spain, a 900-kilometer voyage. The *Camino* ends at the tomb of Santiago-Saint James, and marks a spiritual commitment of the believers to *put their money (actually their feet in this case) where their mouth is,* and take the time and dedication to walk in praise of their Saint, and in service of their own immortal soul.

Pilgrims often suffered deprivations—lack of food, exhaustion, disease, being attacked by bandits along the way, and many other even worse sufferings—but it didn't slow down their numbers or their dedication to finishing their *Camino.*

After her experience of doing the whole 900-kilometer pilgrimage, Marilyn reported, "It was grueling, but the most wonderful and inspiring thing I ever did. I feel like my faith was deepened a thousand times, and felt a sense of personal commitment and dedication like nothing I've ever done before. I now feel like I have the preparation to truly teach and lead youth groups in my church. This was exactly what I needed."

She still feels it was the best thing she ever did, and has continued to think about the influence of that trip, and how it guided her in her life.

Her husband Robert stayed home, worked full time, and took care of their three children the whole time. His comment was, "I'm so proud of Marilyn for doing this. It has been a dream of hers since she was a teenager, and now she did it! Her faith is so much stronger and she's a different, more patient, more forgiving person. I think she was given a miracle on this trip."

She literally became a pilgrim. In many people's lives it's not as evident, but they are still pilgrims. Pilgrims exist as individually dedicated persons within every tradition. They are often highly recognizable as wonderful models of the faith or the tradition. Sometimes they are even seen as saints. They are often very loved and respected as models. If you are one, you will recognize your Marriage Blueprint in the descriptions that follow.

### Living The TRUTH

The ITP Marriage Blueprint relies on tradition but promotes individual roles within it. The individual is expected to seek joy and pleasure within his own world, and find connection to his family (and tradition) through his own personal discoveries.

Sound like you, and your model of marriage? If so, you are Pilgrims. Just like the pilgrims of the Middle Ages in Catholicism, or the devotees making the voyage to Mecca, or Buddhists to Bodhgaya, India, the spiritual birthplace of Buddhism.

Like a religious pilgrim, wearing palm leaves as a sign of his trip to the Holy Land, or one who has made the required pilgrimage to Mecca, or one of the Word on a journey for truth and love who embarks on a dangerous search for a holy relic.

The tradition is there to catch the pilgrim, should he or she fall, and is holding that pilgrim. In the ITP Blueprint, you are on your own while still being in a marriage.

This model is perhaps far less prevalent in the United States than it is in many other parts of the world. Religious and cultural traditions of centuries are still followed with dedication and focus much more in other parts of the world. In the United States, traditions sometimes are easily discarded since we are the "new world," and there's a slant or prejudice toward the "new" in everything.

Thus, the Pilgrim family may feel they are unusual if they are within the U.S.—and they are.

### Not necessarily religious

It might sounds like the Pilgrim is always in pursuit of a religious ideal or in fulfillment of a spiritual practice.

However, his or her "tradition" may very well be something else other than religious. It might be scholarly, it might be an artistic tradition or a sports tradition, it might be from a family history, it might be in running a corporation. But whatever it is, it is a clear and demanding tradition. And if you are part of the Pilgrim marriage, you know what the tradition is, and it gives you great pleasure, focus and joy.

You are directed and focused on your goal, just like the pilgrims of old. You have prayers, meditations or contemplations within you—or other practices which mean as much to you as these activities. Your focus is intense and laser like. It means everything to you, although you would never say that your family or marriage is less important. It feels true and consistent to you.

Your Pilgrim Marriage Blueprint calls for marriage, and possibly family; although the marriage relationship is a place you may not visit much.

You are not expected to stray far from tradition, as opposed to a couple adhering to the "Wild Things" Blueprint.

If you have a Pilgrim Marriage Blueprint, your marriage and family is guided by a tradition, but your own individual expression of that tradition is not only honored and respected, but also expected. It means everything to you, and everyone in your family knows it!

You are on your own to find your own way within your tradition, and to enjoy it on your own.

Individuals within the Pilgrim family may be very intense, focused and driven by clearly defined goals, passion, and even an equivalent ecstasy, transcendence or nirvana in whatever the passion is. You focus on being your best, because it gives you great pleasure.

**The expectation within the Pilgrims' marriage is that each partner will have a burning passion of focus, and that you will have a defined tradition behind it.**

Scientist, teacher, artist, priest—whatever it is, each person with a burning passion, and incredible zeal for the desired goal, though the pathway of tradition, this describes the Pilgrims' Marriage Blueprint.

### Sex

Unless sex itself is the object of the intense focus and passion (not likely, unless you are members of a Hindu Tantric Yoga tradition which has a strict sexual focus and practice), sex in the Pilgrims' marriage is likely to be a rather "dry" subject.

The married couple is likely to spend time as individuals "off in their own worlds," even if those worlds come out of the same tradition. *It's not from lack of love for one another!* It's because of the love and respect they have for each other's unique and valuable time and focus, that they are not very focused on their romantic life together.

It might seem odd to talk of a Pleasure-Driven Marriage Blueprint that doesn't imply much sex, but the pleasure in this case derives from the powerful and passionate pursuit of something else, the obsession with a tradition and its glories.

Don't underestimate the power of the Pilgrim Marriage Blueprint. People connected by their **deep-seated respect of one another** may have the greatest chance of satisfaction in their marriage, and you might be surprised when you talk with them how much they declare their love for one another, even if it doesn't show very much on the outside.

### Parenting and Kids

If kids are part of the picture (and they often will be, if the tradition such as a religious one strongly encourages having children), the **Pilgrim parents are kind, judicious and careful in their rule following, discipline and focus with the children.**

Kids are taught not to bother their parents much with "trivial" things, because the parents are pursuing "important" things.

The model for kids is one of dedicated pursuit, and kids being kids, one might decide to be "just like mom and dad," and be a terrific little soldier in school or sports or other hobbies, and another kid may rebel mightily, and claim their utter cessation from the traditions out of loneliness and boredom.

**Discipline is likely to be cool but firm. The ITP Blueprint person respects individuality!** And will usually see rebellion as part of the process of individual development.

Love between members of the family may be profound and very intense, but it may be expressed quietly and sparingly. Children from these families may later say, "I knew I was loved, but it was seldom said." Part of this is a decision not to place too much burden on children, but to respect their own individuality to grow and develop in his or her own way.

**Harshness, loudness or severity is not likely to be present.** It is probably fairly quiet around the house except for the intense beating of hearts, minds and souls focusing on their individual expressions of—or reactions to the traditions of—the household. It might feel like you can "cut the tension with a knife!"

## Money, And Personal Development

The topics of "Money" and "Personal Development" can't be separated with the Pilgrim family. They are almost the same thing.

Money for education—within the tradition—is one of the most available commodities around. This is the place where you are likely to see the most generosity shown!

For travel, books, art supplies, computers, educational materials of all kinds, there's money (sometimes suddenly appearing) for each person in the family. Above all other things, individuality and the search for passion and excellence within the tradition is encouraged.

The tradition might be art.

It might be a religious tradition.

It might be politics or public life.

It might be academics.

It might be sports.

But in any case, money is to be spent focused on a fulfillment of talent, skill and the pursuit of individual excellence and fulfillment—for the glory of the person and the glory of the tradition.

## Religion and Spirituality

The ITP family may belong to a church, temple, synagogue, mosque, but it's **individual religious worship and one's own spiritual path** within that are encouraged and expected.

Remember the image of the Pilgrim.

Traveling to the place of Pilgrimage to pay homage to the saint, to the Holy Grounds, the Sepulchre, the place of birth of the Prophet.

The ITP Pilgrim is within the tradition, but is his or her own person within that tradition. Not traveling with the crowds, he or she finds an individual, perhaps untrodden path.

This is the speaker in Robert Frost's beloved poem "The Path Less Traveled," which is about a man returning home in the snow at night through already familiar woods, but taking a little different personal path of choice within the familiar woods.

### STRENGTHS of Pilgrim Marriage Blueprint

Individuality and tradition are prized very highly.

So you get two very strong qualities connected with the Pilgrim Marriage Blueprint. A celebration of the individual's own path of passion, seeking and expression. **Deep and very strong achievements are possible through this powerful support of individuality.**

And at the same time a strong allegiance to a tradition and an established Way, which provides *security, meaning, purpose and guidance to the individual.*

Some of the most amazing innovators within science, religion, teaching, art and music have come out of those who are driven by this Belief System's way of framing thinking, feeling and experiencing. It's like a flame is burning on a specific torch very intensely.

### Challenges of the Pilgrim ITP Marriage Blueprint

Sometimes it is hard to get a sense of the real connection of family members, and their feelings for one another within the ITP family, that might be misinterpreted by kids or others as lack of love.

There can be a certain *emotional reserve or coolness* which can be interpreted by outsiders—or even insiders—as a lack of warmth.

The ITP Marriage can, at times, seem a little lonely to its partners. Even though you have a partner who is "good," and who is someone you respect and admire and love, it can feel like you are pretty alone in the world.

If you are a spouse in this marriage (especially if you aren't a Pilgrim type yourself), it can feel a little lonely and painful that all this pleasure and excitement is turned to study, development, innovation or invention; and not to you as a person.

### FACING THE CHALLENGE:

Since all Great Marriages are based on 100% acceptance of self and 100% acceptance of your spouse, your challenge is:

1.  Make sure that you **clearly express your love** for your spouse and other family members, so they don't misinterpret you as being uncaring!
2.  Make sure that others **hear about your true passions, and get a chance to understand you.** Sometimes your focus and passion, appreciated and valued very deeply by you, will be missed by others and interpreted as a lack of interest in them!

### *IF THIS IS YOUR PREFERRED MARRIAGE BLUEPRINT AND YOUR SPOUSE HAS ANOTHER PREFFERED MARRIAGE BLUEPRINT:*

1.  *You might feel that your spouse is "too demanding"* if he or she asks you to "leave off" your pilgrimage for other parts of family life; *recognize that to your spouse, his or her Marriage Blueprint is just as important as yours.* Leave at least a little room for your spouse's expectations and wishes to be honored, just like you would want yours honored!
2.  **Recognize that your ways are not your spouse's.** Be careful to help him or her understand you, and you understand back. It will probably take more time to do this kind of work than you are comfortable with, but it will help you stay satisfied and married in ways that work.

These answers to your challenges are meant as a "starter kit" for you in how to handle differences or conflicts between you and your spouse, or even conflicts inside of you between competing Marriage Blueprints! For more discussion and to get all your questions answered, please visit www.CouplesCoach.com

## 4. "The Big Heart Family"

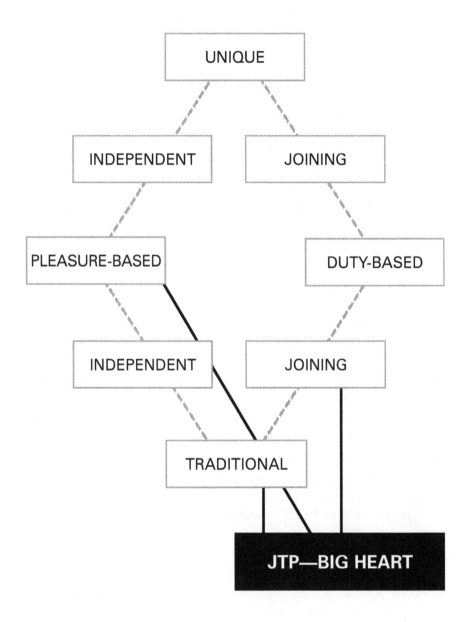

# Joined-Traditional-Pleasure-Based Blueprint: JTP

The "Big Heart Family" is "the family that plays together."

They are "always together," and "always finding something fun to do."

These are very **active families** and very **cohesive** ones. They are likely to be the first ones at the community events, and part of the decoration committee. They are the ones who organize the sports events, the raffles, the car washes, and the Sunday school outings. They host the family picnics and the family reunions.

Theirs is the house where everyone in the community congregates. It's where the tag football games, the Thanksgiving Dinners, the Fourth of July Barbeque happen, and it's where you go after the funeral or the wedding.

They are the ones who buy all the croquet sets, the matched T-shirts with the family slogans on them. They buy the big sets of patio furniture, and (if they can afford it) install the pool in their yard, so all the kids can come to their house.

No one's birthday gets *uncelebrated,* no one is left out of the Thanksgiving Dinner, everyone gets a birthday card and a gift for their anniversary if you are driven by the Big Heart Family Marriage Blueprint!

Affection is forthcoming regularly, physically and verbally. Their motto is "we all love each other," and they feel this tie through their strong traditions and through their connections with one another!

They are the ultimate example of "joining," at least in the most "outward" and obvious form.

The Big Heart Family marriage is about the family and the community. In this sense, the marriage goes out and encircles everyone it comes into contact with.

They have tradition! More than likely they belong to many forms of organized traditions. A church, temple or mosque; community programs for sports teams, stream cleanup, feeding the homeless, counseling pregnant girls; maybe a local music club or country club.

If one learns to play golf, all do. If one wants to see a show, all do. This is truly the "family that plays together and stays together."

## Sex

Affection and warmth are abundant in the "The Big Heart Family" blueprint.

Sex, maybe.

There may not be much time, privacy or left over energy for sex, and it might be put off until "another time" with some frequency. This may or may not be a problem, depending on the individuals and their feelings about this, but it's "part of the picture."

It's not that there tends to be shyness about sex. This is a pleasure driven Belief System! But it's also a Joining Style and very strongly conditioned and driven by tradition.

Depending on the tradition, there may be a lot of strong messages about sex and its place in the marriage, and in life in general. The JTP Marriage Blueprint calls for a real consistency with tradition. So there may or may not be actual sex very much. But there's likely to be a lot of "awareness of sex."

This is a pleasure-driven Belief System, as I said. Sex is part of the pleasurable world. Yet people are around all the time, and the expectation for joining with others is pretty intense.

Sex, when it happens and if you and your partner are in "just the right mood" will probably be great! But you might not get around to it much because of all the other things going on in your life.

## Parenting and Kids

This tends to be a high point and strength of the "Big Heart Family" Marriage Blueprint. The Big Heart Family LOVES kids, lots of them!

The job of the parents is clear. Give your children a pathway into your traditions by making them fun and enjoyable. Participate with them in their learning.

Take them everywhere, and do everything with them. Involve them!

Encourage, show affection and get your children to join in with others!

Children are usually a strong expectation in the JTP Marriage Blueprint. Even if you don't have children of your own, the Belief System holds a strong meaning and place for involvement with children, and helping them grow and develop within the tradition.

## Money

Money's place in the "Big Heart Family's" Marriage Blueprint is to facilitate participation of all members in the tradition, and making it fun and enjoyable.

Money is to be spent on celebrations, anniversaries, weddings, reunions, presents, education and creating a family environment that is conducive to "joining" with the family and the circle around the family.

Money is to be used to "join" people together in pleasure and fun!

## Personal Development

Personal development in the "Big Heart Family" Marriage Blueprint is highly encouraged, as long as it doesn't directly clash with the image of "joining," or take you outside of the tradition.

For example, announcing that, instead of attending college last year, you toured another country—and joined a new religion where you had an affiliation which was very different from the one in your family—would probably be a bomb!

Total silence might descend on your household for perhaps the first time!

But announcing that you had decided to become a _____ (priest, teacher, professor, owner of another franchise of the family business, part owner of the business and manager, etc.) would be taken as a strong and positive move that would be highly encouraged!

A great celebration is likely to ensue upon the announcement of the second option above! And a lot of quiet and consternation on announcement of the first one.

## Religion and Spirituality

The Big Heart Family combines tradition with pleasure, and makes it fun. Religion is part of the celebration of life and enjoyment for this family.

For a long time it was believed that the origin of the word "religion" was *"re-ligare-to join together again,"* as in "reunion,"—and even though recent scholars have questioned this origin, it's exactly what religion is for this family!

Religion is just an ongoing "family reunion," where the family of friends and neighbors gather together to celebrate.

Spirituality is defined as JOINING together. It's a community thing, not a personal search or exploration!

This is the HOME of religion, and where it most fully thrives and has its biggest successes and biggest recruitments.

Traditional religion lives in large part because of the JTP Marriage Blueprint-religion is lived out in the lives of the communities built, maintained, loved and supported by "The Big Heart Family."

## STRENGTHS of the JTP Marriage Blueprint

When you are "in" with the other members of your family (and/or spouse), you feel truly invited and encouraged.

"Joining" is taken seriously, and is a solemn honor.

Almost 35 years ago, I was on a research and study grant that took me to Mexico.

I stayed with a local family for only a couple of weeks, but I felt accepted, loved and cared for just like I was a full member of the family.

Over the years, we have kept in touch through letters, visits, phone calls, and now emails. They said to me at that time, "tu eres familia," and they meant it. One brother who was my age, Julio, joked to me all those many years ago, "If you don't want to be part of this family, you'd better run now and never give a forwarding address!"

I did want to be part of that family, and it's been a great connection over the years.

There is no other place you can feel quite as much at home—if you are "joining" with the others within the tradition of the JTP marriage and family.

The "Big Heart Family" (JTP) marriage will support and sustain you through a lot of turmoil, moments of confusion or loss and betrayal. The JTP family is "there for you"—again, assuming that you are loyal to the tradition and to the process of "joining" with others.

You can have a lot of fun, enjoyment and pleasure by joining with this "team."

This is truly the "team" model.

### Challenges of the Big Heart Family (JTP) Marriage Blueprint

However, should you challenge the tradition or the "team," should you decide to go your own way, you may very quickly find yourself quite exiled, and alienated from the "team."

If you are not "with us," where are you?

On your own.

The biggest challenge of the JTP family is accepting difference. And this Marriage Blueprint is not happy with individuality or difference. This Belief System is based upon "our strength together within our tradition," and, to some extent, on the strength that comes from opposing "others on the outside."

So, if you are now an "other," watch out!

You might find yourself on the outside, and possibly for good.

In other words, individuality is not prized highly within the JTP Marriage Blueprint. Nor is "non-participation." Nor is "questioning the tradition."

This can be a real problem if perhaps you don't much feel like participating, and if you DO feel like questioning!

### *FACING THE CHALLENGE:*

Since all Great Marriages are based on 100% acceptance of self and 100% acceptance of your spouse, your challenge is:

1. Individuality and disagreement! You are so big-hearted that your point of view will often get agreement (because everyone likes your ways and your personality); *you are not used to being disagreed with!* Get used to it, learn how to listen, and to accept other points of view. This will help you a lot.

2. Non-participating. Sometimes, believe it or not, there are people who aren't in the mood for non-stop participating in community events, coming to your house for a party, talking about

everything under the sun. I know, they are party poopers! But insisting when they aren't in the mood—or just for no reason at all don't feel like non-stop participating—won't help your marriage. *Let off the gas* with your spouse when he or she wants to duck out and take a break!

### IF THIS IS YOUR PREFERRED MARRIAGE BLUEPRINT AND YOUR SPOUSE HAS ANOTHER PREFFERED MARRIAGE BLUEPRINT:

1. It will probably seem *amazing to you that anyone would disagree with your way* of "doing marriage and family." After all, yours is one of the closest things to the *ideal* that is portrayed in media, books, movies, and by experts. However, *this can make you cocky and righteous*, and feeling like you have the corner on the market of marriage and family. You don't; your spouse, who has a different view, has a lot to teach you, and I invite you to listen carefully!

2. Use your big heart to embrace his or her difference from you! *You believe in finding agreement and community, and that means embracing difference.* It's good for you, good for your spouse, and good for your community!

These answers to your challenges are meant as a "starter kit" for you in how to handle differences or conflicts between you and your spouse, or even conflicts inside of you between competing Marriage Blueprints! For more discussion and to get all your questions answered, please visit www.CouplesCoach.com

## 5. "The Pioneers"

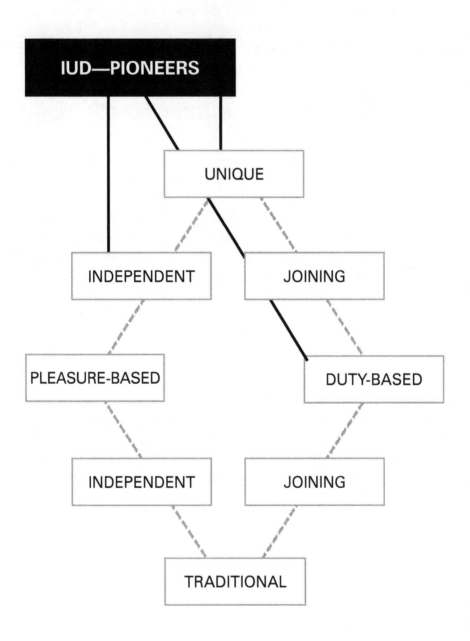

IUD—PIONEERS

UNIQUE

INDEPENDENT

JOINING

PLEASURE-BASED

DUTY-BASED

INDEPENDENT

JOINING

TRADITIONAL

# Independent-Unique-Duty-Based Blueprint: IUD

Now we have moved to the other side of the " East–West" axis, away from "Pleasure-Driven" over to "Duty-Driven" Marriage Blueprints.

This is where we find the **pioneers,** those people who are ready and willing to "go to the mat" for what they believe in, to put their lives on the line and buck the status quo.

Not like the "Wild Things" who as you remember emphasize experience, discovery, newness and fun; but who emphasize the power, majesty and importance of duty to a cause!

On this axis, the driving force is in the service of duty rather than pleasure. This creates a whole different set of conditions. **It has been said that duty is to be useful, not according to our desires, but according to our powers.**

So we've moved away from a model of serving self and pleasure, and into a whole series of Blueprints where the commitment is to a duty.

In this first example, the emphasis is on independent service.

**If you are in a Pioneers' marriage, one or both of you in the marriage has a destiny to serve a cause.** This is the model of the individual pioneer, supported by the one (your spouse) who really understands.

However, this is the unique version of this Blueprint, which means as you know by now that the focus is on a creative and special version of duty.

**The Pioneer Marriage Blueprint requires the special creativity of Individuals within the call to duty.**

The Pioneer has a certain loneliness in their marriage, because he or she is actually serving a duty without an expectation of support or encouragement from others. It would "be nice," but it's not really expected.

This is the lone pioneer who may be "crying in the wilderness." But there's no whining, because this Belief System expects that condition—in fact, praises it.

This is the picture of the "lone inventor," "the renegade and misunderstood artist," and the "pioneer." Lots of rewards if you succeed, always a price to get there. But you don't mind, because the pioneer's path is a reward in itself.

If you are in a Pioneer marriage, you may indeed wonder why you are in a marriage at all. In fact, it may even seem to you like the only reason to be married is for convenience, so that the practical matters of life can be managed together.

**But you really DO know why you are there, because it's a matter of respect and admiration, and doing your best—each in his or her own way—for a responsible and important cause.**

You are each of you a bit like hermit monks of old. It's just "you and God," and your relationship with one another is only (or primarily) on the basis of your respect for one another in the service of duty.

You feel your aloneness, but it doesn't feel bad, since you have your duty to focus on. **This certainly is no Blueprint or Belief System for the weak or faint of heart!** It's only for a stoic and strong person who is utterly committed to his or her cause.

The cause is likely to be something quite solitary as well, such as ascetic prayer, or researching a problem in science, math or engineering, or being an avant-garde artist, or exploring new terrain, or being ranger in remote wilderness where your job is to protect the animals from invasion from poachers, anything where your independence and solitariness is the model you live by.

You are married probably because you finally found someone who seems to understand your Belief System, and what you really and truly believe in, and why you believe in it, one of the few who may ever have understood, and you felt a connection to this person that was special and seemingly uncanny.

### Sex

There may be sex in your marriage, but there may not be much.

Occasionally, for comfort, you may seek the warmth and comfort of one another, but probably not very often, and you may feel in some ways that you have kind of "compromised" your service to your duty, if you do seek this kind of solace.

When I was a high school athlete in the 1960's, our coach was always exhorting us to "stay away from girls" the night before a game.

It was widely believed that having sex within 24 hours of a game stripped a man of his energy and power.

The scientific evidence for this may have disproved its validity, but it wouldn't have mattered to Coach Wilson, I promise you, because his message was clear and unconcerned with science: "Focus on the **game**, and not on your *privates.*"

The Pioneer understands this, because he or she wants to focus on the task!

You may love the person to whom you married very deeply, because of your shared understanding and respect of independence, and why you are together, and what you believe in; and it might even be that you are very active sexually because of this special and rare bond with another who so understands you, and you them.

But pleasure is not "why you are here," so sex plays a minor role in your Marriage Blueprint.

### Parenting and Kids

If you do have children, which is somewhat unlikely, your job is to model for them two things: Independence and service to duty.

You are likely to be very *disciplined with yourself, and pass this on to your children.* This in no way suggests that you are aggressive or threatening to your children (though you may be), but that you are **very focused** on their getting the teaching and the model of discipline in service of your duty.

Nothing would touch you or inspire you more than having your child choose to serve like you! And to do that in his or her own way, with the child's own unique version of whom you are.

You prize their independence and their own ability. You love to see them prove themselves, and show their understanding of making their own choices. But even more than that, you love it when they agree with you on the meanings and purpose of their life.

Your most cherished feeling about a child of yours is that you feel **proud** of them.

You went through that yourself, and disciplined yourself and developed yourself, and it's good to see your children doing the same.

## Money

Pioneers simply don't care much about money for its own sake.

You don't need much for yourself, and although your extreme dedication, creativity and discipline may generate something that has powerful marketability in the rest of the world, that is not your reason for doing what you do!

**Your devotion is to your cause, your research, your art, your purpose, and your duty. When you have that and remain focused on it, you are happy.**

Money that you make will be *directed back* into serving your cause. If you feel you are on the verge of a dramatic new invention, almost all your money will go into getting the materials and machinery to create the prize.

Otherwise, you have little use for money.

## Religion and Spirituality

If you are religious, your religion is your cause, your duty and your calling.

Your Belief System and Marriage Blueprint call for total independence and unique, creative invention of your world within your duty, and a respect for others who do the same.

Because of your independence, you are likely to see little of value in churches or other religious organizations at all, unless perhaps they happen to cross paths with or agree with your independent observations and conclusions.

You might agree with the teachings! You might even be an ardent practitioner of the teachings. But you don't like the "authority" of the church or spiritual practice. Your hard work and devotion give you a better understanding than the church itself or its congregation.

You don't "follow the herd!"

## STRENGTHS of the Pioneer (IUD) Marriage Blueprint

You always have yourself to rely on!

And now that you have an understanding partner, you finally feel like there is at least one person who truly understands what you are all about.

This is great, because it permits you to do what you truly believe in, and to support your partner in what he or she believes in.

You are truly side by side with another person of your mindset.

Actually, your partner doesn't even have to be like you at all. You can respect their difference from you.

What's so important to you is that you have a partner with a feeling of dedication or duty of his or her own.

As for you, you really don't have a lot of confidence in other people's reliability, focus or discipline. Others are kind of "lazy" compared to you.

You aren't relying on other people to remain as focused or dedicated to their duty as you are. You already know that most people don't have the dedication or persistence that you do.

You pride yourself in your independence, your persistence in duty, and your lack of reliance on anyone else; and also in your readiness and willingness to grant this kind of freedom and lack of expectations on other people, and feel that you are generous toward others in this way.

This carries you a long way with your own conscience, and if your partner respects or values you and your focus, you feel like you have found heaven!

---

*It might have taken you a very long time to find this person, and now your appreciation of her or him is very deep and important to you.*

*However, you might not show it as much as your partner would like!*

### Challenges of the Pioneer (IUD) Marriage Blueprint

*It can be lonely!*

*Even the most stoic and "cool hearted," focused and duty driven person, sooner or later feels the lack of other people in his or her life.*

*And when you feel that loneliness, there won't be anybody there. You will probably see that as a challenge and test of your duty and dedication, which it is, but you can't wrap your arms around that and feel connected to other human beings that way.*

> *If you wish to face this challenge, and create more connection and warmth in your life, it can be demanding. For one thing, creating connection and warmth can take a lot of time out of your day!*
>
> *And you really might not see the point of spending all that time and effort.*

### FACING THE CHALLENGE:

Since all Great Marriages are based on 100% acceptance of self and 100% acceptance of your spouse, your challenge is:

1. Make sure you get a *little more warmth and connection into your marriage than you feel comfortable with!* It might seem like kind of a waste of time, and redundant to you (since you'd rather be focusing on your own passions), but it will help create a stronger marriage. And after all, if you have found someone who might understand you this deeply, it would be a shame to lose the special connection. Put a little effort into connecting with your spouse!

2. **Duty isn't everything in life!** Think of it this way: the human body is built in such a way that resting muscles is part of making them stronger. Just ask any bodybuilder. Muscle bulk is built between lifts, not during them—during the "pause!" Having more of what might even seem like "meaningless activity" (i.e. "mindless fun) in your life is a good thing—if only to make you stronger "for the cause."

### IF THIS IS YOUR PREFERRED MARRIAGE BLUEPRINT AND YOUR SPOUSE HAS ANOTHER PREFFERED MARRIAGE BLUEPRINT:

1. This one does not shock you, because "the rest of the world" probably thinks, feels and acts differently from you anyway. You might end up with a familiar feeling of being different. *I encourage you not to just "shrug your shoulders"* at your

spouse's preferences and say, "It can't be helped," but to use a small part of your considerable passion and focus to understanding—and acting—on integrating and participating in the preferences of your spouse!

2. **Be careful not to interpret your spouse's lack of similar interest in what YOU feel so passionately about—and his or her interest in something quite different—as a rejection of you or your own passions and causes!** It's very likely it's only their disinterest in your cause that's happening, not a disinterest in you! You might identify yourself fully with your cause or focus, but your partner doesn't! He or she sees you in ways far beyond your being a pilgrim!

These answers to your challenges are meant as a "starter kit" for you in how to handle differences or conflicts between you and your spouse, or even conflicts inside of you between competing Marriage Blueprints! For more discussion and to get all your questions answered, please visit www.CouplesCoach.com

## 6. "The Visionary Family"

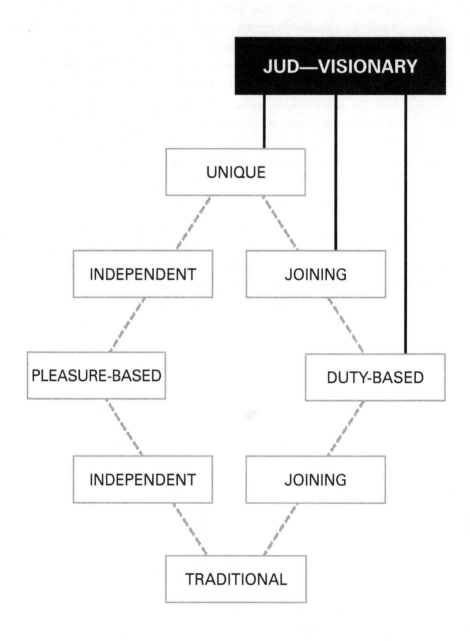

# Joined-Unique-Duty-Based Marriage Blueprint: JUD

In the "Visionary" Marriage Blueprint, you and your family have carved out a unique and powerful devotion to a duty and cause that perhaps few others understand.

But you understand why you are doing it, and you are very *close-knit and focused* on your vision. Your vision is heroic, at least in your mind. Others may not understand what you are doing, or why you are doing it! But you do—and maybe someday they will understand it too. Others might respect you for doing what you are doing, but they are not about to go do it, like you are!

In fact, this is a good image for the JUD Marriage Blueprint: The Visionary Couple or the Visionary Family.

You are *not deterred* from going places together, as a devoted and dedicated couple, into places that might be considered very dangerous or threatening. Contrary to most people and their thinking about safety or comfort, your focus is on being together and joining in your cause, no matter what the discomfort or impossibility of the situation.

Maybe you are even there, or doing what you are doing, BECAUSE of the discomfort or impossibility—and that you realize that only certain people would do such a thing, and those certain people, because of your Belief System and Marriage Blueprint are you and your spouse and family.

You give each other strength to face dangers, threats, as well as misunderstanding on the parts of others. This feels great, to be united in a cause! This sense of togetherness, and having joined together in your duty, gives you a powerful sense of being with your soul mate—perhaps the only person on the planet who could really understand what you two understand together.

You may be living in the service of one or more of many "causes."

- It might be scientific, and you might have a lab where you are trying to work together to cure a disease.
- It might be artistic, where you are working together to create some community art or large scale pieces.

- It might be political, where you are working together for the changes you most believe in, and trying to influence lawmakers and voters for a certain result.
- It might be community-oriented, where you are working for justice within your community. It might be environmental; issues about equality between people; work conditions; religious freedoms; civil rights, or many other things, but whatever it is, your Visionary Marriage Blueprint is *helping you create a unique and potentially very powerful and influential version* of it—if you will apply it with focus and dedication!
- It might be religious—the Visionary Couple or Family is the one who goes on Mission, such as good friends of mine (Alicia and Joe Kitterman) who have decided to live the rest of their lives in a village in Africa serving the poor by providing medical care, and bringing the Word of Christ to them.

It's not that you are "against" the world, but sometimes your kind of "island" existence feels like it. But this only tends to draw you together more.

Your Belief System has these three elements which contribute very strongly to your JUD Marriage Blueprint: "Joining," that is, being together and united; "Uniqueness," or having your own special and different contribution and creativity around what you are doing; and "Duty-based," which means that you are serving a cause that you truly believe in.

When all three of these pieces are running together, it feels to you like you have found paradise! And indeed, according to your Visionary Marriage Blueprint, you have!

### Sex

Sex is an easy part of your marriage to each other. This is because you *already feel so united* and connected, that being sexually connected is a **perfect compliment to what you already feel.**

You probably enjoy sex, but the point is not specifically pleasure as much as it is the feeling of being connected and united in your duty or cause that you are serving.

That feels great, and the sex you have is a natural part of that.

## Parenting and Kids

If you have children, you are most assuredly putting them "to work" in the service of "the cause" or "the vision," and feeling great about that.

**You are feeling great about that since you feel you are giving them a chance to learn something profound, useful and something that helps them find meaning in a special way that so many children never get a chance to experience.**

You are giving your children the kind of *unique and rare education* that can only be provided by people who are willing to go into the crucible together to be forged into greater alloys of the human spirit!

**You expect your children to recognize over time, the meaning and importance of the service you are doing and exposing them to.** You recognize there are many influences in this world, and you are hoping and expecting that your influence will override many of the "lesser influences" that they meet in their lives. Those "lesser," or "inferior," influences are about the masses, and what they enjoy or find captivating.

You expect, from your model, that your children will get outside and beyond these "lessening" or "deflating" models, and adopt your model of joining and duty, and make something of themselves.

You actually expect your children to even outdo you in their creative application of their individuality into the cause or service, where it wouldn't have to necessarily be what you serve, it would be good, since then you could keep connected under "one banner."

## Money

Money goes back into the "vision" or your cause!

You don't want more than survival and subsistence for yourself, your duty to your cause, and having the chance to be together in the service of duty, is blessing and value enough for you.

**If you can generate a significant amount of money for the vision, this will make you quite happy and satisfied, and pleased that you have contributed a lot, and done it together.**

## Personal Development

Your personal development in the Visionary Marriage Blueprint is all about becoming a better servant to your cause.

The primary method of personal development is study and focus on the traditional sources of wisdom—whether those be in the wisdom books, or the teachers, or your own prayer and meditation—it depends on the tradition, but whatever the tradition teaches is where you get the personal development. One should always be developing personally, but in the Visionary Blueprint it is according to the definitions of the tradition.

And the purpose of personal development is to become a better servant, and easier to work with—more cooperative, more understanding, and more accepting of others.

And more patient and focused on your duty and its achievement, and with the cooperation of others!

### Religion and Spirituality

**Religion—or in the Visionary Marriage Blueprint, service to a cause with discipline and duty—is already "hard wired" into your Belief System.**

Nothing more is needed.

You might be working with organized or formal religion already, in connection to your cause or duty, but if you are not, you might as well be.

In your own life, the "cause" you are serving IS your religion, no matter whether it is formally connected to a recognized religious organization or not!

### STRENGTHS of the Visionary (JUD) Marriage Blueprint

You are right where you believe you should be—working together, and working on something you really believe in, and using your creativity and personal drive to achieve something worthwhile.

The fact that you have company, and like-minded others working alongside you, helps you not get caught in the feeling that you are totally alone in the world.

You have a soul mate!

You have someone who understands your unique, and perhaps quite quirky views and unusual dedication and duty to a cause. It's not "the norm" to be the way you are, so it is nice to know that you have this connection to another, and to a "family" of others who share your focus and duty.

## Challenges of the Visionary (JUD) Marriage Blueprint

It's going to be a crushing blow to you if your soul mate (or other family members) gets a different idea, and decides to go "join another team," one other than yours!

It's going to be even more crushing if the "team" they join is the one you are struggling against.

This happens more frequently than you might like!

Or if they just simply *don't feel* like doing it anymore. Often people run out of gas (or confidence or drive), with a dedication to a cause, and years of constant struggle. Maybe your partner isn't as clear, strong or dedicated as you, and their sense of duty is not as strong as yours.

It's possible their vision is a Personal Marriage Blueprint that they took on in order to be with you! In this case, it might not be able to stand up to the constant battering that "serving the cause" can take.

Being in the service or duty of a cause—or a purpose in life— sometimes just gets too tiring or boring for some people, even if they have a Belief System that tells them that this is the "right way to live."

You may have to face this some day, and it might feel like a profound disappointment, or even a betrayal to you. Your challenge will be to find a way to accept and love his or her difference from you, if you are going to have a Great Marriage.

### FACING THE CHALLENGE:

Since all Great Marriages are based on 100% acceptance of self and 100% acceptance of your spouse, your challenge is:

1. I repeat from above: It's going to be a crushing blow to you if your soul mate (or other family members) gets a different idea and decides to go "join another team" than yours! It's going to be even more crushing if the "team" they join is the one you are struggling against. **Answer: I know, HOW COULD THEY DO THIS TO YOU? Well, the point is, it's not being**

done to you. Others may simply see things differently! I know, how could the do this to you? Honestly, it's not personal. Seems like it, but they just changed their mind! It's OK. Just keep on doing what you do so well.

2. And I repeat this also: Or they just simply don't feel like doing it anymore. Often people run out of gas (or confidence or drive) with a dedication to a cause, and years of constant struggle. Maybe your partner isn't as clear, strong or dedicated as you, and their sense of duty is not as strong as yours. **Answer: Just take it easy, and stop expecting so much of them. They might just need a break!**

*IF THIS IS YOUR PREFERRED MARRIAGE BLUEPRINT AND YOUR SPOUSE HAS ANOTHER PREFFERED MARRIAGE BLUEPRINT:*

1. This can feel crushing and personal. The most important thing is to realize that simply because your spouse wants different things from what you do, doesn't mean that they don't love you, love who you are, or value what you stand for. **It may simply mean that they have a different point of view from yours.** That understanding will get you a long way toward feeling better about your differences.

2. Focus on what you do, and do it well. **Your spouse will respect you and value what you do, even if they don't agree with you that it's THEIR way of doing things.** Your spouse having a different set of preferences is NOT a personal attack on you, so don't take it as one!

These answers to your challenges are meant as a "starter kit" for you in how to handle differences or conflicts between you and your spouse, or even conflicts inside of you between competing Marriage Blueprints! For more discussion and to get all your questions answered, please visit www.CouplesCoach.com

## 7. "The Golden Rule Family"

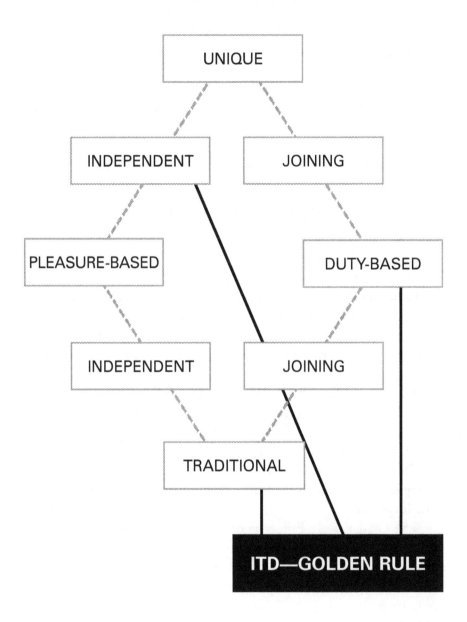

# Independent-Traditional-Duty-Based Blueprint: ITD

If you get on an airplane, you definitely want to know that your pilot lives by this blueprint.

If you go in for surgery, you'd feel far better if you knew your doctor followed it. Your dentist, accountant and your kids' teachers? Yes, please, make sure this is their blueprint!

Oh yeah, your minister, rabbi, guru. Better have it.

The rock musicians you see in concert? Nah! Gimme the Wild Things! ☺

## The Essential Golden Rule!

Most people believe in the Golden Rule, "Do unto others as you would have them do unto you."

Others may *believe* in it, talk about it, or even *consider* it one of their important values. The Golden Rule Family makes it the **center and guiding principle of everything they do!**

Everything a person does in this family is measured against this guidance, and your worth is determined on how well you meet this standard.

The Golden Rule Family Marriage Blueprint calls for individuals to live in the service of tradition and duty. Roles and expectations for each person are clear. They are defined by the traditions that are being served. Please, no wiggling around; the path is clear!

The combination of duty plus tradition means that the "servant" is very focused on defining proper application of the service, and the duty it calls for.

The Golden Rule Family is one that focuses on order, structure and service. You don't have to necessarily be a minister or one of these other professions mentioned. Whatever you do in life, it will be driven not only by standards, starting with the Golden Rule, but also other values as well.

The key words are:

- Tradition
- Order

---

- Duty
- Service
- Individual meaning and purpose

Properness is very important in the ITD marriage and family.

**Propriety, care, thoroughness and follow-through** are of principal concern.

If you are in an ITD (Golden Rule) Marriage, you know it! You couldn't help but know it, since your role is defined and very specific. You know what you are supposed to do, and that your **individual responsibility** is the point.

You know you will be judged, and will judge yourself, on the basis of your performance and consistency of performance of your duty within the tradition you serve.

For example if you are a teacher who has this Belief System, you will evaluate your job on the basis of whether you properly presented the material, kept an orderly class, and got good behavior and high grades from more students than not; you are not going to be concerned or interested in how many offbeat, wild-eyed geniuses you inspired, unless you inspired them to become better, and more proper, citizens.

**The Golden Rule Marriage Blueprint is one whose principles apply to everything you do, whether your profession, friendships, parenting, or marriage.**

You are individuals who value respect, kindness, thoughtfulness and moderation in your relationship with each other. These things rank very high on your scales of evaluation, and if they are lacking or instead represented by crudeness, self-centeredness or excess, they will get a very bad "grade" from your Belief System!

**"A place for everything and everything in its place,"** is a motto for your Marriage Blueprint. It's how you run your house, your conversations, your finances, and your time. That includes people, big and small. Each and every person needs to know what their place is, and not be too eager or expecting to change that place, but find pleasure, contentment and satisfaction in it.

When "God's in his heaven and all is right with the world," and such order is in place, it feels exactly right to you. **Your Belief System calls for order and you expect it.** Your Belief System calls for service to duty and you expect it, both from yourself and from other people. *Your Belief System calls for an acceptance and honor paid to what you call tradition, and you expect it—both from yourself and from other people.*

## Sex

You may think of sex as a proper expression of love for one another between two people. Your sexual relationship will tend to be very considerate, and probably not very experimental or "wicked" (though people who know you might be VERY surprised if they knew what goes on in your bedroom!). If your tradition teaches it, you may think of sex as a wonderful sacrament and a joy given by the divine for our enjoyment of one another.

And this is fine with you.

You may see other people in the world obsessed with sex, and caught in what you view as terrible addictions, and pain of captivity to substances, bad habits and ego. You hate to see it, and wish you could do something for others who are caught in such ways by their addictions.

Your Belief System teaches you that each individual is responsible to himself or herself—and to your tradition. Each individual answers for his or her ethical and responsible practice of gratefulness—and no "ego"—in the service of tradition and duty. Marriages and families that follow this view you respect, others you do not!

Sex is thus a proper and good part of marriage, but not something that you tend to obsess about. If you find yourself focusing on or desiring sex beyond that, you are likely to feel angry and disappointed with yourself, and admonish yourself to "straighten up" your behavior, thinking and feeling—to be more in line with your Belief System.

## Parenting and Kids

Children are to be directly and clearly taught the rules.

Kids **KNOW the rules** in the Golden Rule Family.

Children need refining until they can become mature and developed; they will get honed in their lives through experiences and opportunities to practice the right way to live.

Kids are wonderful gifts to us, but they need direction, guidance, care and focus in order to "grow straight and tall."

Good parents make sure that their children get proper instruction, and then they expect their offspring to conform to the traditions and their duty in their young lives as quickly and thoroughly as is possible.

### Money

Money exists to serve duty and tradition.

It's perfectly acceptable to have financial security, and even wealth, if a good portion of it is properly directed. Otherwise, it would be considered as excess, pride and ego.

When you have money, part of your obligation is to share it. Golden Rule Families are good tithers to churches and contributors to charities.

But they also give their time, and consider that as good or better than money. Money is only one way of contributing, and the Golden Rule Family believes in contributing, and puts their money and time where their mouth is!

### Personal Development

"Man is never perfected."

What this implies in the Golden Rule (ITD) Marriage Blueprint is that each human person should always work to better himself or herself, continuously and without ceasing.

**The source that should be consulted in personal development? Your tradition.** If your tradition is Christianity, for example, it's obviously The Bible. If it is Buddhism, the Diamond Sutra or other teachings. Or the Koran, the Talmud, the Tao Te Ching; whatever are the core teachings of your tradition!

If the tradition you serve is excellent education, then you study the best in your field. Same with sports, art, business, creative writing, welding, medicine, or whatever it is that you practice, and is your field of focus, and your tradition.

**You view yourself as always developing, and always in need of further molding and perfection. You can never be perfect, but you can work toward perfection.**

The Belief System drives this, because your goal remains perfection, even though it is unobtainable. You know this, but you still pursue it.

Why? Because your feeling of worth and value completely depend on it.

## Religion and Spirituality

If you follow a formal religion, you will be very **loyal, faithful and dedicated** to your religion, if you have the Golden Rule Blueprint (ITD).

This means that each of you in the marriage is expected to be true to your tradition, and to your duty, and to do the best you can to follow that tradition.

It's a mutual expectation—and the expectation is very strong, and the judgment rather severe (at least in the opinion of others about you within this Marriage Blueprint).

## STRENGTHS of the Golden Rule (ITD) Marriage Blueprint

Clarity!

You have a clear set of standards to follow, and you know instantly and with certainty whether you have followed them or not.

There's little guesswork on your evaluation of yourself about these expectations, standards and your performance. **You are responsible yourself,** as an individual to your duty and your tradition, and you don't have to wait around and really figure out whether others will approve of you or not. *You know if you have "done your job" or not.*

You can have a strong sense of security in knowing what (according to your tradition) is right, and what is wrong! That helps your feeling of wellbeing, and being "at home in the world."

You know that you have a longstanding tradition, and that millions of people have gained meaning, solace and purpose in life following the traditions and duties that your Belief System guides you to follow.

You have history on your side as a helpful guide to your actions!

## Challenges of the Golden Rule (ITD) Marriage Blueprint

**Your conscience can haunt you relentlessly!**

And you can begin *judging* your spouse or children with respect to whether they are holding to the standards.

And then, you wouldn't be practicing the Golden Rule! Because you wouldn't be treating others as you would be treated.

You and your spouse may disagree about the standards or definitions of the rules. Uh-oh, this is going to be a values conflict!

Since you can never fully "measure up" to your standards, there's always at least some vague feeling of failure that you face with the Golden Rule Blueprint.

Have you been a good spouse, a good person, a good father, a good mother? Have you been a good model to your children and others?

Have you let yourself, your tradition and/or your duty down? Are you worthy?

These kinds of thoughts, anxieties and worries can end up being paralyzing and de-motivating in your individual, as well as in your married and family life.

If your spouse disagrees with you about how to live, for example if he or she has a very opposite Blueprint, such as the Wild Things (to take an extreme), you may be constantly in turmoil about how to respond.

Your spouse isn't following the rules! What are you to do?

## FACING THE CHALLENGE:

Since all Great Marriages are based on 100% acceptance of self and 100% acceptance of your spouse, your challenge is:

1. **Recognizing that other people may not be as rule or principle —driven as you are,** and that NOT being rule-driven is just as valid a way to live as your way. Find ways to be accepting of this difference from you and your preferred way.
2. **Take it easy on yourself.** You already know you cannot be perfect, so why not extend a little more compassion to yourself? "Do unto yourself," also!
3. More fun and enjoyment would do you some good; you might be too serious. You wouldn't deny people you like their fair share of fun and enjoyment, why shouldn't you have a little more yourself?

*IF THIS IS YOUR PREFERRED MARRIAGE BLUEPRINT AND YOUR SPOUSE HAS ANOTHER PREFFERED MARRIAGE BLUEPRINT:*

1. The importance of your standards for yourself might blind you a bit to the fact that yours is only one way to see reality. **Consider your spouse's difference from you as the test of your own character!**
2. It could be of great benefit to you to really study some of the other Marriage Blueprints, and *compassionately imagine* how it would be to live by them. Whatever your spouse's preference is, if you put your considerable skill and intelligence into it, you'll be able to really *understand the wonderful challenge* that has been given to you to develop yourself as a human being by having this difference between you! Fortunately for you, the 8 Marriage Blueprints have already been outlined for you, so here's your manual for practice right in front of you!

These answers to your challenges are meant as a "starter kit" for you in how to handle differences or conflicts between you and your spouse, or even conflicts inside of you between competing Marriage Blueprints! For more discussion and to get all your questions answered, please visit www.CouplesCoach.com

## 8. "The Royal Family"

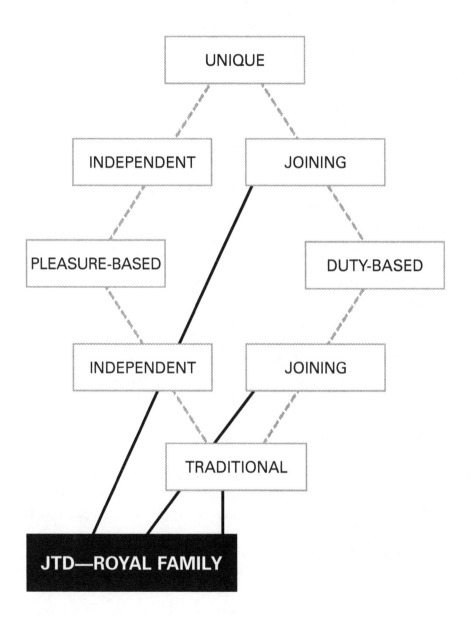

# Joined-Traditional-Duty-Based Blueprint: JTD

Is your calling to be a model couple or family to your community?

If so, then you will identify with this Marriage Blueprint!

The "nation" or the "kingdom," at least of your house, family, neighborhood, town and community (as far out as you can handle) is your audience, and those for whom you are modeling your Blueprint!

It's a Blueprint that calls for public display and community involvement!

Many years ago when I taught at a private prep school, the headmaster and his wife were what I would now consider a powerful model of the Royal Family Marriage Blueprint.

You rarely saw either Mr. or Mrs. Showalter outside of one another's presence. They represented the school—and its wealthy and influential parents—at public events both within the smaller community, and within the city where we lived.

This was a very highly regarded school, where many of the most prominent citizens of the community had gone to school, and it kept up relations right through the running of major corporations, political organizations, state government, and even up to the national level.

This headmaster and wife conducted themselves in such a way that when they walked into a room, one had the *sense of perfection, properness, and all the circumstance that goes along with fully groomed and "finished" society.*

This image was not an accident. It was clear that Mr. and Mrs. Showalter had been carefully educated and guided into these roles which they played to perfection, and that there was a precise match between who they were and the positions they represented.

The Royal Couple feels this strong combination of many expectations and requirements on who they *are* and *should be* in their marriage and family.

If the Royal Family Marriage Blueprint (JTD) drives you, you have a lot of standards coming at you from *both inside and outside!* You have an expectation of "joining," so that you both are on the "same page" with your expectations, Belief Systems, thoughts, feelings and behavior.

---

You had better be, anyway! Your public will expect it! You'd better perform!

You promote, support and represent your tradition—together. This means knowing all the rules, laws, history, actions, and presentation of self, both inside and to others.

A high level of *scrutiny can come down on you* both from inside your own judgment, and perhaps from others, if you should fall short of meeting these standards. And you expect both individuals to be in sync on your meeting these standards.

You have an expectation of meeting your duty, and must continuously evaluate yourselves as a married couple and family, to make sure that *everyone is joining together, following tradition and performing their duty!*

Sounds like a lot to keep track of to most of us, but perhaps it sounds just right to you—and a wonderful challenge. The rest of us admire you!

The Royal Family Marriage Blueprint is one of high standards, but it is also one that can receive *very high rewards!*

Many of our biggest leaders in business, professions, public speaking, ministry, politics and many other fields do their best to represent a "united front" or a Royal Family image to the public, and their best imitation of an actual royal couple. This is a powerful and magnetic image to us even in an era of "democracy," that a Royal Couple might be in power, endowed with special powers and charisma.

So if you are a "Royal Couple" (even if it's just in your neighborhood or church, it doesn't matter), this Blueprint brings on big scrutiny with the potential of big indictment, but also with the possibility of massive rewards and power.

It's exciting and seductive, and only a few people can really "pull it off," although many are driven by this image of themselves!

### Sex

It's been said often that *power is the strongest aphrodisiac,* and many people long to have this charisma, and to be regarded as important and powerful!

Is literal sex actually involved in this charisma? Sometimes. More often than not it is the "idea" of sex that is even more appealing than sex itself. Being "sexy," being "appealing." Honestly, his or her sex life is not any better than anyone else's, although the myth seems to imply it is. But who knows?

After all, it's often been said that sex is all in your head, and that the biggest sex organ you have is between your ears!

You might feel the rush of energy "between the ears," which can drive an exciting sex life. If so, *good for you*. But don't be surprised if the "sizzle" doesn't match the "steak." The point of the Royal Couple is to create a good "outer image." If you have done that, **you've done plenty!**

But then again, if it's not working perfectly, your sexual relationship itself might suffer quite a bit. It's a gamble, this "getting it all right" thing. When it works, it works powerfully, and you feel very potent. When it doesn't, it's very easy to end up feeling very impotent!

### Parenting and Kids

Children must, of course, be instructed in how to be "part of the scene" or proper followers of tradition, duty and the family.

Their instruction must be very thorough, if they are to "represent" the family and the tradition.

I don't mean to imply that the family "actually" has to be royal, wealthy or powerful. In many middle class families, there is still this sense that the family is representing something very important, deep and traditional, and that the children are part of the "image of the family."

Being a proper family, and representing it is a skill. You understand how it should be done—just right for your own community (no matter how large or small), and you know how to "pull it off." Your kids must be instructed in "the way."

Thus, kids have to be prepared, educated and finished for public consumption.

Education of children must be "in the tradition," and of the proper kind. They need to be taught a sense of duty and service, and **how to be a representative of the family at all times.**

Some kids can pull this off no matter what the circumstances since they get so good at "representing" the image.

Some very wealthy and well-educated kids (Ben and Rudy) I know regularly get stopped by the police, and never get tickets even when they have alcohol and drugs in the car.

Ben and Rudy are *"good."* They have the "look" and presentation of the powerful "Royal Family" about them, and this way of presenting oneself is very powerful in the world.

On the other hand, the kids from another similar family I know, are some of the best models of achievement, tradition and pride to their family and community that they can be. They are using exactly the same tools, but to different results. They are actually using the tools the way I think their families meant them to be used.

So raising kids for the Royal Family is a tough job. You have to find the balance between promoting a feeling of "entitlement," and a feeling of "responsibility." Spoiled or respectable and praiseworthy? How will they "turn out?"

This can be a very good thing for families and communities since "royal kids" can strongly and positively influence their peers, and are some of the most powerful influences kids are going to have in their lives.

Tough job, helping them to make those distinctions.

Others don't envy you trying to make these subtle distinctions with your children.

### Money

Money in the Royal Family (JTD) Marriage Blueprint is regarded as a tool to an end, which is proper "royal" representation of tradition, family, duty and certain values.

Money is very useful in "tailoring" your image to be exactly whatever you want it to be, and JTD Families learn how to use money to do exactly that.

Money can help promote a strong community and a strong public awareness. Your responsibility is large, and much will be asked of you!

You have both great rewards and great responsibilities, and you are called upon to exercise wisdom and conscientiousness in the execution of both!

## Personal Development

Personal development in Royal Family (JTD) families is directed toward service to tradition, duty, family and even community, state and nation if the level is high enough.

**Public service, leadership skills and knowledge are the focus of personal development,** no matter on which level it is exercised (could just be among peers, or in the home, or in the church, or sports team, or it could be on the level of state, national or international government!).

It's preferable to go to the best and highest rated university possible!

So personal development is strongly encouraged, or even required, as long as it serves these kinds of leadership goals.

## Religion and Spirituality

Religion and spirituality are often extremely important in JTD families because formal religion and its structures are often the foundation and focus of the tradition and duty of service that are taught in JTD families.

You are the representative of your "people," and you take that seriously.

*Formal structure, rules, guidance and direction* are very important in the Belief Systems of Royal Families. And religious organizations are, of course, natural sources for these kinds of structures. So the alignment tends to be very fortuitous and congruent. It is another place to look good, to shine and be noticed—and to fulfill your promise!

## STRENGTHS of the JTD Marriage Blueprint

The strengths of this Marriage Blueprint are the same ones as the traditions on which it might be built, since the expectations and practices of the Royal Family are almost a direct "manual" of the tradition, with little deviation expected or allowed.

**Others are looking to you for guidance, so you have a great opportunity to lead—and the preparation to do so!**

Thus, a member of a JTD Family has a clear and detailed manual of the proper thoughts, feelings and behaviors that are to be followed in this Belief System for success and wellbeing.

Because of this clarity, a person might feel very secure, directed, and have a sense of destiny and purpose, as well as the roadmap of how to fulfill that destiny.

If you are a member of this kind of "Royal Family," your course—should you choose to follow it—has a strong and vibrant future!

### Challenges of the JTD Marriage Blueprint

For anyone with a streak of true rebellion in him or her, the JTD Blueprint can feel incredibly **stifling and strangling.**

The expectations and rules are *staggering.* The expectation of continuous and precise actions and behaviors can potentially be overwhelming—especially if you don't like the rules or the expectations!

I know of several cases where the weight of these expectations—and the duties and traditions of this Belief System were so great—that children were overwhelmed and either strongly considered suicide or carried it out.

In one case in which I know the family, the son did actually kill himself, leaving a note which said, in effect, "Dad, I can't meet your standards and must get out of the way of this family."

Interestingly enough, the family turned it into a positive, and started a foundation for "confused kids."

For most Royal Families, the benefits and potential rewards may vastly outweigh the challenges and expectations.

But if you won't conform and "play ball," you and the whole family are in trouble, and solving that trouble can be very costly and energy sapping.

### *FACING THE CHALLENGE:*

Since all Great Marriages are based on 100% acceptance of self and 100% acceptance of your spouse, your challenge is:

1. Many people will put your family under **extreme scrutiny.** You will have to be prepared for criticism and potential negativity, and for meeting it with graciousness, warmth and understanding.
2. Your expectations are so high! It's a good idea to think carefully about how seriously you want to take yourself as a Royal

Couple or Royal Family. **What are the consequences to your family?** Would you be perhaps happier and enjoy life more if you were able to loosen up and take it easy?

3. Your Blueprint doesn't allow much individuality! Would your children or spouse be **happier** if they were encouraged to have differences of opinion?

*IF THIS IS YOUR PREFERRED MARRIAGE BLUEPRINT AND YOUR SPOUSE HAS ANOTHER PREFFERED MARRIAGE BLUEPRINT:*

1. This is not easy! You have such a public image expectation that it might be difficult to accept if your spouse is totally uninterested in performing according to your standards. **You will have to decide whether being the Royal Family or having a Great Marriage is more important to you.** I mean really think about it. It might be a "one cancels the other" decision.

2. Can you be **less demanding** on your spouse, and let him or her have as much involvement in working for your tradition or cause as is possible? Can you allow more **"time off"** for your spouse from "the cause?" He or she might be more likely to want to participate if allowed to have more latitude and feeling of personal wellbeing!

These answers to your challenges are meant as a "starter kit" for you in how to handle differences or conflicts between you and your spouse, or even conflicts inside of you between competing Marriage Blueprints! For more discussion and to get all your questions answered, please visit www.CouplesCoach.com

# CHAPTER TWENTY-ONE

## How to Supercharge your Marital Happiness And Rediscover the Sizzle!

So now that you have the 8 Basic Marriage Blueprints in snapshot form in front of you:

1. "Wild Things" (Independent Unique Pleasure-Based, IUP)
2. "Bliss-Mates"(Joined Unique Pleasure-Based, JUP)
3. "Pilgrims" (Independent Traditional Pleasure Based, ITP)
4. "The Big Heart Family" (Joined Traditional Pleasure-Based, JTP)
5. "Pioneers" (Independent Unique Duty-Based, IUD)
6. "The Visionary Family" (Joined Unique Duty-Based, JUD)
7. "The Golden Rule Family" (Independent Traditional, Duty-Based, ITD)
8. "The Royal Family" (Joined Traditional Duty-Based, JTD)

Let me go back to the questions I asked you to consider before I started describing the Marriage Blueprints and their qualities, strengths and challenges. Your questions to ask yourself are:

1. What is my Family Marriage Blueprint—which of these 8 is the closest to my own earliest version what marriage is and what it should be?

2. What is my Personal Marriage Blueprint—which of these 8 is the closest to what I NOW think marriage is and what it should be?

3. What is my spouse's Family Marriage Blueprint—which of these 8 is the closest to his or her own earliest version of what marriage is and what it should be?
4. What is my spouse's Personal Marriage Blueprint—which of these 8 is the closest to he or she NOW thinks marriage is and what it should be?
5. Which of these 8 is the closest description of the Marriage we are ACTUALLY LIVING RIGHT NOW?
6. How close or far away from the two Blueprints I have for marriage is the marriage we are actually living right now? How true is this marriage to what I expect and think it should be?
7. How close or far away from the two Blueprints my spouse has for marriage is the marriage we are actually living right now? How true is this marriage to what he or she expects and thinks it should be?

And, by now, I am sure you have very good answers to these questions. Let me ask them in a much simpler form.

1. Do you like your marriage as it is today?
2. Which model or blueprint do you wish it were more like, if you don't like it?
3. Which model or blueprint does your spouse wish it were more like, if he or she doesn't like it?
4. If you or your spouse would like a change, what will it be and how will you make those changes without changing who you are?

---

**When looking at the 8 Marriage Blueprints:**

- What would you like? What appeals to you? Is it what you already have, or something else?
- Did you know you had these choices, that there is not only "one way" to be married, or live a married life, but rather a complete menu, from which you are totally free to make your choices.
- What would you like? What would you prefer if it were "no holds barred?"

- What would your parents like you to choose?
- What would your friends like you to choose?
- What would your religious teachings tell you to choose?
- What would your local culture and neighbors tell you to choose?
- Which Marriage Blueprint excites you the most?
- Which scares you the most?
- Which sounds most interesting?
- Which sounds to you like it would make the best life for you and your spouse?
- Which sounds like it would be a total disaster for you personally?
- Which sounds like it would be a total disaster for your spouse?
- Which sounds like it would be the biggest change for you from where you are now?
- Which one is your "secret desire" Blueprint?
- Which ones have you already "tried out" with other people? How did that work out?
- Which one is most like your parents' marriage?
- Which one is least like your parent's marriage?
- Do these questions excite you? Scare you? Threaten you? Thrill you? Bore you? Challenge you?

There are a lot more questions, and a lot more answers to those questions about Great Marriages and great family life at www.CouplesCoach.com.

**Did you ever think there was this much variety in Marriage models?**
You now see that you truly do have choices about what you want to adopt as your Belief System or Marriage Blueprint, and that you can actively initiate change simply by changing your beliefs about what is possible, and then acting on those changes.

You might be thinking right now that you have found much more freedom in actually thinking, feeling and believing about what marriage and family are—or can be—than you have ever known in the past.

This freedom allows you perhaps for the first time ever in your life to feel that your life can change spontaneously—and change for good—deep inside, to the kind of life you would really like. And you can have the great marriage you always dreamed about.

Isn't it nice to know that many people already have the kind of marriage that you might like, but in some ways never suspected or dreamed was truly possible? But now you see it might actually be possible. It IS possible to have a life and a marriage that you want, you desire, you long for!

You might find that a whole new way of viewing marriage is evolving inside of you spontaneously; and that some of what you are discovering surprises you! Maybe you didn't think it was OK to have the kind of marriage you imagine. But now you see that the varieties of marriage —of Great Marriage—are many, and that only your imagination limits what is possible. This means that if you expand your imagination, you also expand your possibilities. And expanding your imagination is what you have done by reading this book!

## Your Partner Might Have Different Blueprints

It can happen that your partner has quite different Marriage Blueprints than yours. It's not even rare, but happens all the time.
For some reason we have been taught that agreement is necessary for marital happiness. But now you know this is not true. What is necessary is to solve the Intimacy Paradox, that is, 100% acceptance of yourself and 100% acceptance of your spouse.

You know that what this takes is lowering your defenses and seeing differences as not only acceptable, but the deepest truth about human existence. In fact, our differences are what make us real spiritual beings and infinitely interesting to one another. Don't minimize the differences between you, glorify them!

It's so good that now you have found in your mind, heart and soul that there is so much room for all of these thoughts and differences, and that we can all fit in this world—which is even bigger than you expected in your wildest dreams—those dreams which even now are beginning to come into view, and to find you. Just as you are finding them.

It's not too shocking to discover that your partner is someone different than you thought they were now that you understand this, is it? Didn't you discover in reading this book that you yourself were different than you thought you were, and in fact, you didn't even know yourself very well?

You now understand that if you are living in a model of marriage which you don't like it might be because your Family Marriage Blueprint is in charge, and is not how you would like to live. And that what is necessary is to shift that energy that is bound up in that old Belief System into the new one you are forming. How do you shift it? By stating the new beliefs, writing them down, and seeking evidence for their truth!

When I said that you may have "shrunk the marriage" by cutting off your communication and narrowing what is acceptable in your relationship, I wanted you to understand, and now I hope you do. What is necessary for a Great Marriage is that you enlarge your marriage. Make it even bigger than it ever was before! The way you do this is to lower your defenses, open up your success channels, understand your Marriage Blueprints, and build as big and important and deep a marriage as you can. You deserve a true marriage, a deep and extremely satisfying marriage, and I've shown you how to get it and keep it. Go boldly!

I conducted a marriage ceremony for two friends a while back and this is what I said about marriage: "Marriage is the best chance we have to truly know someone and truly be known by someone before we die." Don't blow your chance!

If you are going to be married with someone, be married boldly and with courage! Truly get to know who that person is, and what he or she authentically thinks, feels, believes and values. And also, while you are at it, truly know who you are, what you think, feel, believe and value.

Why be alive at all if you are not going to boldly explore who you are and what you are doing? Live fully and genuinely, whatever your Belief System, and whatever your Marriage Blueprints happen to be.

We talk a lot about freedom, but how many people exercise it in the places where it most matters? Are you truly exercising the freedom to live out who you really are, and to put that true self in front of the people you love? Or are you simply biding time and waiting around—for what?

Each of these Marriage Blueprints is nothing but a pattern people have already lived by, and ways they have loved each other deeply—just ways and thoughts and actions, which are neutral until you assign them meaning. Something in one or more of the Blueprints will have touched your own nature, your desires, and your longings. You might feel that you would really like to live your life and in your marriage the way the Blueprint describes. But maybe you haven't felt permission to live that way since it seems counter to the way you believe you should live.

Well, if you are looking for permission, go ahead and take it. Grant it to yourself. There's no reason to be nervous about change, and there is every reason to just go ahead and be who you really are and really want to be. Go for it!

I have shown you a map of your own brain, your own thoughts and feelings, and what drives your actions. I've shown you a map of marriage and all the places on that map. You have the option of going anywhere you like on this map whenever you like. The secret that few people really understand is that you are indeed completely free to choose how you think, feel and act.

Now when you are sad, you know why you are sad. When you are happy, you know why you are happy. When you are angry, outraged, calm, bitter, excited or having any other feeling or thought, now you know why! Everything that happens inside of you and in your actions is driven by the engine of your beliefs and their "evidence seeking mechanism."

All the data that comes at us from the world is neutral until we assign it meaning.

And it just comes down to making choices on the basis of that neutral data and information coming at us—to just put it in the funnel you decide to throw it in, and fill up a jar and keep filling it up.

*Fill it up, fill it up, fill it up.*

You don't have to change who you are to have a great marriage.

And that's all there is to it.

# CHAPTER TWENTY-TWO

## A Free Gift for YOU!

### Other Resources, Free Gift
### More Ideas and Help on Using Your Marriage Blueprint

Thank you for buying my book!

**And thank you for all you are doing to have a Great Marriage.**

I have a free gift worth $49.95 I would like to give to you!

Please go to this web address to get your gift: www.MarriageBlueprint.com/gift.html

I want to help you **personally** in your progress forward with your marriage. This is why I have created a special relationship questionnaire for you which will help you

- Nail down your own preferred Marriage Blueprint
- Know how best to succeed and be happy with this Blueprint
- How to handle differences that may come up between you and your spouse
- And how to use this information to have a Great Marriage!

After finishing the questionnaire, you'll get your **personalized** special report immediately.

You and your spouse should each finish the questionnaire separately.

You can also get answers to other questions you may have about creating a Great Marriage and great family life, and find other very valuable resources at this website: www.CouplesCoach.com

Isn't it nice to know that the marriage you always dreamed of is right here at hand?

Grab it!

*Dr. Max*

# About Dr. Max

Dr. Max Vogt – *"Dr. Max"* – gets results!

He is a very unusual Couples Therapist and California-licensed psychologist with over 25 years experience helping people finally "click" in all aspects of their lives.

Why "unusual?" Because Dr. Max not only helps people get results. He helps people get amazingly *rapid* results—and, those results *last!*

His courses, books and videos will help YOU create true confidence in life.

Dr. Max's materials will show you how to:

- Create Incredible Relationships
- Generate Quick and Easy Life Plans and Goals
- Unlock Your Money and Finance Power
- Rediscover a Spiritual Life That Brings You Sheer Joy
- Get in Shape, Stay in Shape—and ENJOY it!

Dr. Max is widely published both in print and on the Internet. His totally unique, powerful step-by-step approaches to people's most important challenges have transformed the lives of thousands of men and women around the world.

If you are ready for a change for the better, why not make it happen now?

**To visit Dr. Max on the Web go to:**

www.AskDoctorMax.com
www.CouplesCoach.com
www.MarriageBlueprint.com
Great FREE articles about marriage:
www.YourMarriageAdvisor.com

You'll find a LOT of fantastic information, with much of it free. Enjoy!